THE
BOOK OF
BROCK

**Brock Hilditch
and
his Ma, Val**

Balboa Press books may be ordered through booksellers or by contacting:

Balboa Press
A Division of Hay House
1663 Liberty Drive
Bloomington, IN 47403
www.balboapress.co.uk
UK TFN: 0800 0148647 (Toll Free inside the UK)
UK Local: 02036 956325 (+44 20 3695 6325 from outside the UK)

ISBN: 978-1-9822-8721-4 (sc)
ISBN: 978-1-9822-8722-1 (e)

Print information available on the last page.

Balboa Press rev. date: 07/11/2023

Dedicated to my Great-Grandaughter Fiadh Kirkham

Afterword

My motive for writing this book was curiosity. How would the world look through a dog's eyes? especially one who is not very tall! I thought writing this might bring a smile to people's faces. What started with posts on the Sealyham Appreciation Society Facebook page of Brocks daily antics, has grown massively and following the feedback I have received, I wondered if I could write a book – and here it is : The Book of Brock. Enjoy.

7th September 2021

Well, I am absolutely shattered. Ma had top behaviourist/psychologist man in today; have to admit she did need it. When I greeted him, he sprayed a nasty smell on his clothes, so I didn't bother jumping up. Then we proceeded to do training stuff. Ma bit slow, but she'll get there. I helped her out by pretending to be good and obedient 😇, escaped to the bedroom whilst they were talking behind my back—rude so I thought I would take apart a pair of Ma's glasses 😅. The fun part was when he bought his collie Bruce in, who proceeded to steal my toys 😳😵; I didn't mind as I am good like that. Take me ages to get over that session. Just hope Ma's learnt something useful 😖 and two hours later he went and I collapsed asleep.

8th September 2021

Just back from late walk, cos of the heat. I had to protect Ma against a huge snow leopard following us. She tried to tell me it's only a cat, but I knew better; seen them on that talking pictures machine in the corner. Anyway, I saw it off—think that bossy man's training went through the window at that point. Know Ma's really shaken as she's having a glass of something she calls her medicine 😅😅😅. Me, I'm not stupid; I'm a Sealy, and it's really called wine 😂🥴. Give me a bone any day. Brock signing off; have a good evening, all.

9th September 2021

What a walk, guys; met lots of puppies. The *really* exciting bit, though, is about corpses. I saw a great big sewer rat with snarly mouth and teeth. Ma had to drag me past, as I wanted to start a collection at home in my museum of dead things. Next thing, before you know it, a great porcupine squashed in the road—but would make a good exhibit. I have just been told off by Ma for exaggeration. She said it was a shrew and a hedgehog 😵😆. I didn't correct her, but Sealies were bred for hunting. I do know my prey 😆.

11th September 2021

Flat-out eventful evening last night, I went outside as usual but found a huge hairy tarantula. It was as big as my paw and had huge long legs and red eyes. I had to bring and show Ma; she ought to know what is lurking in my garden to keep her safe. I was duty bound to devour it in front of her, one leg dangling out of my mouth and tarantula juice dripping from it onto the carpet almost dissolving it 😆. Oh lawks alive. Ma's just caught me with her phone and told me to tell the truth 😌. She's such a spoilsport. Okay, garden spider, but it was big and hairy. Sooner I can have my own mobile phone the better 😆.

16th September 2021

Brock here. Got Ma's phone, so can post in peace 😁. Have been with my Labrador stepbrother's great craic. I showed Cooper, my best friend, up to Ma's bedroom and we raided it. Spoils of war—trainers, spectacle case, mankie-looking sock 😆. Let Cooper have that (hee-hee). Then, lawks alive, the excitement of it all: we had aliens probably from Mars right outside the window, and their spaceship made a bleeping sound. All we could see were white domes with yellow jackets going up and down the road, hundreds of them. The hedge was in the way of their probably webbed feet and scaly legs—truly terrifying. But I reassured Monty (black Lab and leader of the pack) and Cooper (fox red Lab) and visitor George that I had special connections in the Sealy world 😎 and that I would sort it out with my superior intelligence—that's what our breed is world renowned for.

Uh-oh—lawks. Here's Ma, scowl on her face. Okay, so they were only tarmac men, not aliens with white hard hats on. Spaceship was their big lorry. But I really did lead a raid on Ma's bedroom. I am the leader of the pack really; just let Monty think he is. Ouch 😆. Ma's just nudged me. Okay, I'm the bottom of the pack—at the moment cos I'm only one and exaggerate most things. Greetings from Brock.

18th September 2021

So Ma had a day playing the leader of the pack yesterday 😁. We were all good; I only led Cooper on a few bedroom raids (should close the door). Great haul: mobile phone, hairbrush, and yet another trainer, which enabled us to get cheese in exchange for each item. Not daft am I. Riotous games in the garden and then collapse in our beds to get energy up for more pillaging. I liken us to Viking raiders: Cooper the Red and Brock the Bearded. (Monty the Black is above all our games; doesn't know what he is missing.) X big sloppy kiss from Brock the Bearded and greetings from Cooper the Red.

20ᵗʰ September 2021

Here's me after my hols with Ma and the Labradors. Can't believe it, but this morning, lying on Ma's bed (mine, really; I let her share), I heard a huge rumbling and saw lights flashing. It was really scary, but I jumped up to protect Ma. It was the mother ship that had tracked me from Lincolnshire. (I told Ma it was a spaceship, not a tarmac laying lorry outside our house there). It came rumbling very slowly, searching, seeking me out, lights flashing on the roof. I expect they wanted to pupnap me and experiment to see how we Sealyhams are so darn clever. I let it rip, yelling at it, and it eventually rumbled off.

Uh-oh, here she comes correcting me 😳. "Road-sweeper, Brock. Don't exaggerate again, or I will have my phone back dadedadeda 😩." Chap can't have a bit of fun these days. Well, time for another sleep. Been on the go 24/7 with Cooper, so got to get my strength back. Brock checking out. xx

24ᵗʰ September 2021

Can you see this this is a game changer for me—saved Ma's life. I told her there were black panthers around. I saw it looking at us ready to pounce on us and rip us limb from limb. I gave it such a look, frowning as hard as I could. On closer inspection I had frightened it to death; it was rigid. I have the stare of death—useful 🐶. Uh-oh. Ma's looking over my shoulder. Okay, okay, this time it was a black metal cat scarer, but next time, who knows when I can use my newfound weapon, "the Sealy stare of death". I will probably be sent to war-torn countries to use it.

30ᵗʰ September 2021

Just having forty winks before I create evening havoc 😴. During walk this morning, fighting a hurricane, I told Ma to hold on tight and I would keep her safe 😳. Responsibility on my young shoulders anyway. I was in search of the elusive fox poo which my mates tell me it's great to roll in. My mate Cooper who I stay with sometimes can sniff it out in seconds. Ohhhh, he smells sooo good after, but no luck today. I didn't see any vultures either; too windy, I expect. OK, kites, is that better? So home for coffee and my pathetic crumb of biscuit.

This afternoon I was left all alone to take care of things, which of course I did, and made an amazing discovery. The big long box on the table that Ma puts water and green stuff in is not empty; there is a prehistoric monster in there looks a bit like a crusty pork pie with scaly legs. With the unlikely name of Miss Ziggy Stardust. She's in there cos I read her post the other day calling me an exaggerating pup 🙂. Well, I'm not letting on I know; it's our secret, but the cheek of her. 🐶 Well, I've been around the room like the wall of death, hundreds of miles an hour, jumping from sofa to sofa (I should go to agility classes). Now quick rest, calm before the storm 😴🐵😇. Have a quieter evening than we are going to have 😴😂.

1ˢᵗ October 2021

The worst has happened. I always admire the handsome Sealy in the other little oven-like thing in the grate. Horror of horrors—Ma's set fire to him! I stared at him, but he just stared back. Flame's licking around his legs and body … strangely unperturbed. Maybe he's not a Sealy but what they call a hot dog 😵. I checked later when the flames had stopped. We wagged tails together, so all good there.

Afternoon walk sooo wet I needed my snorkel 🐊 🐳. Onwards we waded. No tigers lurking; too wet for them. OK, Ma, everybody knows I mean cats 😵. Only met a little Westie, nearly as wet as me. For once didn't mind the stupid coat, really, but what's this sprouting out of all my pores, Ma? It's called a *coat*. In fact, Sealies have double helpings, so do we really need dressing up 🙁? Brock over and out. xx

2ⁿᵈ October 2021

Well, what a night 😵. Garden was invaded by a giant porcupine. I went out for a wee, and lawks alive, it scuttled behind some pots. Well, of course I let rip. Ma went mad shushing me or trying to. Ohhh, I could cut my teeth for hunting training on this prickly creature. No, out comes Ma and forms a barricade to stop me getting it. OK, hedgehog, Ma; happy now? OK, small hedgehog 😊.

Found out I have a fetish 😕 🫣, or so Ma said. Just can't walk past a car without a good smell of the bumper. I can find out if there is any roadkill there. Ma said not to worry; teenagers often have fetishes, and mine is quite innocent, and I will probably grow out of it. Just going to have a nap now to energise myself for the rest of the day 😴.

5th October 2021

Brock here. Well, no intruders in the garden last night; too wet. Before my walk just checking; the beautiful Sealy is still safe under the hedge with the sheep. Sure enough he wagged his tail just like I do; could swear it's a mirror image 😲.

5th October 2021, continued …

Had a lovely day. Morning walk, had wrestle with beautiful blonde Piper; came half out of my harness. Ma to the rescue. Then this afternoon wrestling with Tilly, the beautiful Newfoundland, though she lies down so I can jump on her head. She's lovely and soft to lie on.

Ma's groomer came today, and I was sooo good; no barking and jumping up, as Ma was brandishing the tin plate and metal disc things "Bossy Man" gave her. Groomer was amazed at how good I was. Ah well, like to please some of the time. Saw my pug friends too, so our Ma's had natter—and then home for dinner. Yum, liver on kibble. Looking out for giant porcupine again tonight, as dry so far. xx

6th October 2021

Well, guys, had a great walk this morning. Met a minuscule puppy. Ma said it was a cheewahwah, or that's what it sounded like. Pure black and as big as my paw 😳. I was very gentle with Luna (that's her name), so after that met another friend, Daisy. I could see a lady in her garden watching me, so went to say hello. I did my commando walk all the way to her (that goes down sooo well). She was lovely and made a big fuss of me. Then another lady came out, so more commando crawling and more fuss-bliss (I will have a bald chest at this rate). Then around the corner and men in high-viz jackets (do love a bit of high-viz like my collar and lead). They were in ditches behind a yellow plastic fence—but know what, I was invited around to look down the ditch and had *another* fuss made of me. What a lovely walk.

Then high alert: saw the postie's cart, but you've guessed. It was the "I don't carry any treats" man. Lawks alive, what an old misery guts; hope he doesn't get his ankles bitten—not by me, of course. Met a tiger cat stalking me, so turned and gave it my best Sealy killer frown, and it shrunk back into the undergrowth 😆. All this, and still got afternoon walk; bet that's a downer after this morning. The only thing I didn't think of much was loads of big sacks in lots of drives. I was told very firmly no watering to be done on them, as Air ambulance collection. Think a bit of Brock sprinkle would have only enhanced them, but hey, Ma said *no* 🙄. Best to let her think she's the leader. Bossy man said she had to assert herself, so I play along 😂😆. xx

PS: I am thinking of trying a bit of poetry—another string to my bow, and apparently it's in the family, as Ma's grandad was a poet (amusing type) and short story writer for Liverpool *Echo*, Victorian era, whatever that was. Ma showed me all the books of press cuttings she's got, *definitely* not to be chewed. His moniker was Tedimus H. Maybe Brockster H would suit me 😆🙃. xx

7ᵗʰ October 2021

This afternoon Ma brushing up leaves, me helping, when hello, wait a minute. I can see something in the honeysuckle hedge. Ma's had a look and says it's my imagination. Well, I know I have a very active imagination, but there is definitely something spying on us, ready to attack and rip us limb from limb. The sparrows all live in there, but I can see evil red eyes watching us. It's probably a spy from Russia. After my messages from my dead letter box (which was empty today), it probably knows I'm undercover disguised as a pet Sealy instead of an international Sealy superspy. Life is so complicated.

Told you afternoon walk would be boring, and it was, apart from some rabbit Maltesers. Had a good mouthful before Ma caught on 😆😂, and that, my friends, is that. Oh, apart from Ma's friend's letter came through our door. I thought it was my fan mail, so tried to rip it open; got flea in the ear about that—not literally, you understand. No, well protected in that department, as I hope we all are. Scrap that last remark; sounds too righteous 🙄😎.

18ᵗʰ October 2021

Yes, I have been bullied and harassed 😔 by my own Ma. Dragged—yes, dragged into downstairs loo room and forcibly held while she washed my beard. Ruined it and my rep. I don't seem to have any rights around here. I know she will be trying to get tags, etc., out when dry. Groomers next Monday (I'm good for her 😆) and this nonsense can stop. Signing off, a very hard done by and disgruntled Brock. xx

PS: Just got back—one and a half hours traipsing about in the rain; now thoroughly soaked. Ma needn't have bothered 😂😆🐶🐶🐶.

22nd October 2021

Hi, guys. Well, this afternoon Ma and I came across this strange stuff on the wall. There was another skeleton thing as well. This used to be a nice town. It's now being haunted; not so sure about this. We passed the cattle market. That was deliberate; you know how Ma loves her cow smells (still trying to figure out the remark "bought up with cows when little in Wales" ☺). Says it takes her back to her Welsh nanna. Was she a cow too? There were sheep there in the market. Ma said, "Take a good look, and never chase them," as I would be shot by the farmer. As if I would ☺. Well, I had to drag her away, filling her lungs with cow smells, embarrassing me. It's *me* that should do the sniffing.

Ma took me out last evening, when it was nearly dark, as she had been shopping—spending my pocket money, I suppose. I was told to expect deer in the fields and maybe foxes and bats. Umppp; one pesky cat on a fence last time I went out that late. Didn't even see my hairy rat ☺; always tomorrow. I know its address: third tree on the left by the horse field so paws crossed. ☺☺☺

PS: They are bombing us now ✻ ✻ ✻. Who? you ask. Well, aliens, of course. They have it in for me and my super-Sealy powers. Lawks alive, like being in a war zone ☺. Here she comes ☺. "Brock, for goodness' sake, fireworks bangers." I was too young to bother last year. Apparently, it's going to get worse. Well, I want a crash hat to wear, just in case, until all the explosions are finished. Door under the stairs could be left ajar. If Harry Potter could live under the stairs, it's good enough for me to use. I am well read, and Ma tells me a lot ☺. xx ☺☺☺☺

26th October 2021

☺☺☺☺☺☺ Yeah, circus comes to town ☺. Brocky the Sealy packed his bag and ran away with the circus ♫♫ just like Nellie the elephant ☺. I've never seen a circus before. Ma explained in her garbled way ☺ what it's all about; sounds sooo exciting. Lots of people could laugh at me (Sealyhams are the clowns of the terrier group). Well, can't see me on a trapeze; legs too short, and would need a leg up. Rather spoil the effect. Not supposed to have animal acts anymore, so bang goes big cat training with my super-Sealy killer frown—though dead cats not much of an act. Sooo stuck with the clown ☺ label. Told Ma I could sit and beg give my paw, sit, lie down, and do magnificent commando crawling. Very unkindly and quite rude, I thought, I was told that is not much of an act—and no, not being taken as not allowed in the big top. So cunning plan; some might call it blackmail, but packed my case right under Ma's nose and threatened to run away with the circus if I didn't get my own way. Do you know what she did? She helped me pack ☺☺. Lawks alive, my cunning plot gone south, backfired on me ☺. Will just have to dream about going to the circus ☺. From one very sad Brock ☺☺. xx

28th October 2021

Well, saw lots of things today. Looks like the circus has got clowns already ☹😃. There were tarantulas in a web; that was scary. The webs were nearly as good as in our house 😸. Then I found a great stick and decided I would whittle a flute out of it so I could play for Dylan the pug while he serenaded me. What happened to "It's your walk; you enjoy it. Time is yours"? Hmmmmph. Ten minutes whittle time, and that was it. Marched off, leaving unfinished flute on the grass. See if it's still there tomorrow.

On the way back through town the library had put books outside. Was told not to wee on them; better manners than that 😸. Anyway, read most of them; avid reader me. That's where I get my super-Sealy knowledge from. Had a few games with pals on the way, so home for dinner—yum. Quick snooze 😴 and then up and at 'em by the time Ma wants to watch TV with a glass of medicine 😋😃😃😃. Enjoy your quiet evenings, one and all. xx

29th October 2021

Hi, guys. Just looking at the rain, waiting for it to stop. When I got out, there was a huge flashing lorry (😳 you know my first thought: aliens tracking me—yes, obsessed; I know). On closer inspection, they had a huge crater (oh, okay, Ma—a hole). I thought they were digging somebody up who had been concreted over by the Mafia 😬. You hear about that, but Ma said, "Pull yourself together; it's a drain." Rather spoilt the excitement. Ma's grandson, Tom—well, grandman, as very tall—and his girlfriend Emma, and Ma's daughter-in-law, Lon came visiting. Ohhhh, it was lovely. They loved me. I did Sealy commando crawling, begging, etc. They had never seen a Sealy before, so had to impress as acting ambassador of Sealies (save our breed). Sunny afternoon walk and ready for dinner 🥣. I gave up using the spoon. xx

31st October 2021

Well, guys, another spooky walk on Halloween night, in the twilight at the end. Not used to walking in the twilight zone 😳. Found this beautiful huge branch of willow blown down—well, nearly half the tree—and was I allowed to drag it home? *No*, I was not! I promised to be *really* good for the rest of the week, but Ma not having any of it. She said it looks like a stockade already on our drive and doorstep, and how is that my fault when I can't bring them in? Saw some more pumpkins; we have been invaded with them. Probably tiny micro cameras and spy stuff inside them disguised as seeds. You will see; they will all disappear after tonight. Mother ship will be hovering over us while we are in our beds. I will definitely have one eye open ◉. Last scare was a huge ghost 👻 flapping about in the wind. Nah, didn't frighten me, but I had to drag Ma away; could see she was scared. The saddest part of our walk: I watched the circus packing up to go out of town, and I never did audition as a 🤡 clown. Never mind; I'm going to learn to walk on stilts, ready for next year so will only be half-unpacking my suitcase.

On our way home I did find a green-faced clown, also sad to be leaving 🙁. She said she would miss my schnozzle (👃). All's not lost; we exchanged peemail addresses, and she's going to be my paw-pal, and we will send each other peemails.

😔 Never walked in a hurricane before. It was exciting—here she comes. High winds, then—okay, Ma 😵. She's gone now; really was a hurricane 😷🥴🤡. xx 🥺

PS: It's started already. Rockets and fiery trails and bangs in the sky. I'm being good and keeping stum at the moment.

31ˢᵗ October 2021, continued ...

This morning's walk: hazardous. Broken branches down, lots of storm damage. Men up on roofs everywhere. Walked quickly past, as so windy still, and didn't want a man on my head. Don't think Ma wanted one either. Poor old dear; past all that 😷. Met some new friends, and we had good games. I was spoilt for choice with all the branches down, so dragged one along until a better one came along. Mother ship must have come last night. Orange heads mostly beamed up with their knowledge. I put my nose into so many, they will have close-ups of my big black Sealy nose. So I will have to be cautious; don't want to be beamed up for experimental purposes.

Going to snatch some 😴 to ready myself for rest of the day. Have a good one, and be careful of falling branches. I can't be everywhere at once to arrive with my super-Sealy cape on to rescue you all. Short-pawed, and service is stretched at the moment. Got to start recruiting. St Bernards and their brandy kegs would be great, although a bit slow. xx

2ⁿᵈ November 2021

Well, lawks alive. Silly o'clock there. I was fast asleep in our pit (winter duvet on; really bouncy. Mmm😴). Then suddenly Ma gets up. sliding out of our pit, but of course😳 with my superpowers I am wide awake and at heel—the only time I am😂. I know exactly the problem: she has heard you can make money from blogging. Well, I warned her, I'm not helping her. (Don't know this blogging, only bragging. Quite good at that 😄, and there it ends.)

Well, she signs up, pays thirty quid, and is signed up for blogging—and then doesn't know what to do. That is Ma to a T. She likes to think she's up with the kids. but 😵, oh lawks, tears ahead, I fear, and her son's eyes rolling, saying, "Ohhh, Mother, now what?"

Anyway, I sneaked up to our bedroom and found an old suitcase under the bed😳😳. Must be secret. Well, Ma's a dark horse. I found secrets 🤫🤫🤫🤫 her close friends know, but she hadn't told me, probably because I'm a blabbermouth. She lived a life before she had me, in a flat in the 'sixties in Liverpool—something called beetles era. (Yuck; sounds awful. I eat them given half a chance.) Was one of the first wags whatever that was; probably had a tail like me, although she tells me, brought up with cows in a place called Wales. Strange Ma I have got 🥴, and went out with Ian Callaghan, who played for Liverpool football club. Then she went out with *Clockwork Orange* star Malcolm McDowell while he was studying drama at the Liverpool playhouse and used to listen to him practicing his accents etc. for his exams although at that time he was Malcolm Taylor and worked for Maxwell House coffee. You see there is a chance for me and stardom yet. and I'm sure I'm better looking than the lot of 'em. Ma just confirmed I am the best.

Then she went through various channels and became director of Jim Clarke—the best formula one racing driver (Ma just said when it was skill not engineering that mattered; ooohh, hark at her) motoring shoe who she appeared to have a great time with. Poor Jim; she said he was a lovely person as were the others saw his tragic demise in her scrapbook. She lived between Wellingborough and her office in Italy and the Paris branch, where the motoring shoes were made, so Ma went to France too, but sadly before my time. But don't forget: I have sampled escargot à la Thrapston 🤢 and pretended to like it, smiling at Ma with the juice dripping down my beard as I crunched it (secretly, yuck—first and last one).

Well, I think Ma is tiring now; about blinking time too😄. You can tell how tired she is not looking over my shoulder now so bloody hell! Tee hee. I heard somebody say that. Shhh 🤫. I will get told off tomorrow. Ohhhh, lawks alive, it is tomorrow now 😵😵😵😵. Too late now to retract her secrets. People will have to probably google people mentioned, as they are antiques like my Ma. I do love my quirky strange Ma, though, very much 😄🤍🤍. Hope you all have had a more peaceful night. xx

Brock signing off, dragging Ma to bed.

3rd November 2021

Well, what a cold day. Thank goodness I've got two coats. We did a big walk this afternoon. I found this very interesting branch on the ground. Ma said not to eat the berries. Saw some orange heads, obviously left behind when the mother ship came to beam them up; probably rejects. Two had had a fight; lawks, their heads were squashed all over the road.

Then Ma and I walked past cattle market. I let her take me as I know what she's like with cows; sadly only 🐑 sheep today, which quite frankly I prefer. So Ma had a face on her for a while. On the new estate we cut through my fave, as big machines working there—yellow ones with big buckets on the front (Ma told me not aliens just construction machinery). I had to stand and admire them for ages. I really, really wanted a ride in the bucket, but Ma said, "Think again, sunshine," which I thought quite rude thought she could have at least asked a man. Feel quite sorry for the men working there; their heads are such a funny shape and coloured yellow. Maybe that's what you have to look like to qualify to drive those machines. I don't even with Sealy superpowers think I can get my head to look like that. 😔👷

5th November 2021 (Bonfire Night)

Hi, guys. Busy day. Ma's son over this morning. Love him to bits. Then went visiting afternoon and played with Edie until she got cranky. I called her cranky Scottie, which she thought was a great compliment. Mollie was much nicer to me likes me to kiss her. She's a good-looking sprocket but older 🙂, so I have to be gentle and respectful. That's difficult, but I manage it. Walking home, met pretty Yorkshire terrier with three ladies. I charmed them with my best Sealy commando crawling. they laughed so much, of course I did it even more 🐶🐶🐶 (could include that in my circus routine if I can't manage the stilt walking). Further on past the CLOSED pet shop I met a very young Alsatian puppy. Ma remarked, "Don't often get all black Alsatians." 😵 How embarrassing. The owners said, "Oh no, he's blue." 😳😖 Oh, Ma 🤭 (he looked black to me too😋). We had a little play. Had to be careful, not too boisterous. Blue dog's orange pumpkin invaders confusion reigns😆. Dark now, so got to get into my protective clothing etc. to protect Ma and that stuck-up secret from me 😒 tortoise, Miss Ziggy Stardust. Bombing started—stay safe. 🐶🐶🐶🐶🐶🐶

7ᵗʰ November 2021

Hi, guys, Well, I am eaten up with fox poo envy. I had decided they were extinct. Ma's friend got up at five a.m. yesterday to let my pals out, and she came back into the house and thought what a dreadful smell 😷😂😆. Yes she had got fresh squashy fox poo on her slippers and trodden it through (sorry I laughed). Annoying thing: when I visit her garden, zero results. No wonder, now that she's keeping it all for herself. Sadly, when I next visit, expect she's scrubbed all the beautiful aroma away ☹. I'm doomed to never have a roll in said smell. Did get some delicious rabbits Maltesers the other day before I was hauled away 😒. Met my lovely gentleman friend who always makes big fuss of me, then thanks Ma. Had a real fright on our walk. Ma suddenly made this screaming sound. I kept an eye 👀 on her after that; kept having a quick sideways look. She laughed and said it was only a sneeze. Lawks alive; humans make the scariest noises.

14ᵗʰ November 2021

Went in the car to visit Ma's friend who's moving soon so I had the run of the house. Couldn't drag myself away from her bedroom. Lawks alive, she's got the most beautiful Sealies in there, remarkably like the ones in our oven glass and fire stove thingy glass—even outside in the garden, things mirrors (think they are called) have them looking out at me. *Never* do they play with me; just stare at me. And the one in the 🔥 fire doesn't mind getting burnt. Really worried first time I saw him peering through the flames, but he wagged his tail.

Then funny noises, and a herd of bullocks had got into the field by her garden. They were jumping around, chasing each other, joyful. Hilarious, I thought—Ma's friend not so amused. So today was more interesting than I expected 🐮🐮. Prancing bullocks 🤡🤡 —what fun.

16ᵗʰ November 2021

Another stick, another walk; the longer the better, on both counts. Yesterday I was happily shuffling through the leaves in the park when I rooted up an exquisite bone. Really old and smelly. I trotted on, then Ma saw a part hanging out of my mouth. She tried to wrestle it out of my mouth; did my best Sealy wriggle, tossing my head from side to side. Well, it was a real tussle, I can tell you. Then a Mr Nosy Parker came over and offered help; saying he didn't mind if I even bit him 😳😃. Lawks alive, I'm not an animal—oooops, forgot; I am actually 😃😃. Anyway, he crouched down pulling, and I pulled even harder. Ma was trying to open my mouth, then foul play: Ma put her hand over my nose, so had to open my mouth to breathe. Shucks, I lost my bone. Mr N P won. Ma was very grateful and thanked him very much; hmmph. By the way, no humans were harmed in this incident.😃

This morning saw some scary dangerous swan things flying, bigger than the vulture kite things. Had couple of friendly tussles with some of my mates, and back home for coffee ☕. Not for me, thanks; small Scotch will do me fine 😃😃😃😃😝. xx

16ᵗʰ November 2021, continued ...

Hi, guys. Well, short post tonight. Disgusting start to my day. Up dead of night, five a.m., dragged round the block. Then a man shining a torch came down my drive. Well, must admit I warned him off, but out Ma goes. Complete stranger, but there she went. Adrian, her son and my hero, came over to take me a daylight walk and then brought Ma back. Well, lawks alive, what did she look like 👀🐷? She had a patch over her eye. I got a blow-by-blow description of how a surgeon cut her eyeball open to put a new lens in😫. So I read up and am now qualified Sealy eye surgeon. I am going to be putting her drops in for her, so no worries whatsoever; in very safe paws 😹😹😸😸😸.

20ᵗʰ November 2021

Fabulous treat. Went to a Sealyham meet-up in Fineshade Woods. Thousands of us there. OK, Ma 😌, over twelve. Auntie Jenny took us, as Ma not allowed to drive yet. Found two had come from my Essex birth home so probably related. I didn't have to use my super-Sealy killer frown, not once, as all well behaved. Didn't see any hairy rats in the trees either. Nor any vultures circling. Ma calls them red kites; ahhh, as if. I'm not daft; kites are what kids fly on long string. Going to have a quick nap now; energise myself before dinner. Lovely to see you guys 😸😸😸😸. Thanks for organising it, Eddie.

22ⁿᵈ November 2021

Campanology practice. Can't have a pee in peace in my own back garden, so came right back, barked at Ma in protest, threw myself down, shuddering sigh. Drama school taught me a lot; they said I was very promising. At least the bells aren't so loud in here. I know Ma likes the clanging noise, but lawks alive. Just saying😸😸.

23ʳᵈ November 2021

Jiggered. Interesting morning. We met two people who Ma knew, but they moved to Scarborough (she's enough to make you move somewhere—but I love her), and they had come visiting. Another of Ma's friends with lovely silver hair. I thought she had magic powers, but Ma said it was Christine and not magic. There was me waiting for her to do a trick 😕. Then, god help me, the two ladies, one who's not magic, and Ma all started talking cataract operations, as they had all had them. Why do humans always talk about joints and bowels and operations? I never mention my brush with death on the operating table. OK, Ma, it was all straightforward, demasculating me (without my permission, I must stress), but I didn't sue 😫. Anyway, I had a good nose into the silver-haired not-magic lady's house, as front door open. Think I've got interior designer genes. Ma tried to wash my beard, but as she is not allowed to bend down yet, she didn't stand a chance 😹😝😸😸 😂. xx

24ᵗʰ November 2021

Got cornered and was trapped in downstairs loo. Yup, beard washed, but made sure that the floor was soaking wet. Good job for Ma it's tiled. Shame really, as mate I met today was having a really good snuffle in my beard this morning, probably looking for bits of my breakfast maybe. No chance of that 😹. Met a tiny teacup Yorkie baby this morning 👀. What's that all about? Do humans drink out of her? No saucer in sight, so incomplete; must research this. Do they have dinner-plate dogs? Very strange.

Ma has put Xmas decs up. Didn't dare last year; I would have eaten them—might still do. No expense spared; three wooden drummer boys and a large silver soldier 😂🙃and that's it. Ding dong 🐼🤡🐼.

24ᵗʰ November 2021, continued …

Hi, guys. Well, cold walks today. Pesky 🐅 tiger/cats stalking around, so my super-Sealy killer frown was getting used a lot with the occasional Sealy yowls. Saw more dangerous swan things. One came out of the water and hissed at us. I jumped in front of Ma to protect her, regardless of the threat of being beaten to death by its wings. And as for the molehills, they are mountains. Must be giant moles, so I dampened them down 😆 Wonder if I wet their heads.

I got told off by Ma as I tried to take a stick of a small person. Well, he was waving it at me, so I grabbed the end and tugged. He tugged back, shouting, "It's my stick!" I thought what a great game, but no, I was in the wrong. No surprise there🤡😆. What a palaver thought; you're welcome to it. Shook my head and strutted off to find a wonderful prize: an empty shiny packet. So turned into Womble mode and started to do some litter picking very community-minded, me, as I am self-appointed neighbourhood watchdog (good excuse to be nosy). Stay warm; at least I'm lucky enough to have two layers of coats 🐼🐼.

29ᵗʰ November 2021

Well, soooo excited. I knew I was different. I'm a Magical Duke. I asked Ma to show me my pedigree, and there it was. I'm now going to learn some tricks—not my normal ones. Sleight of paw sounds attractive to me. Might learn to saw Ma in two as well 😆🐼. My blood must be blue, as I'm royal. I wonder what number I am in line for the super-Sealy ruling king job. I can't do everything, though; already neighbourhood watchdog/carer for Ma/and secret agent / oh, forgot the consultant surgeon thingy as well; although haven't practiced much on that one. Amazing, really, that I have packed all that in my short life. Sealies are very clever and are first-class clowns, so I think that's why we are a rare breed. Too many of us, and we could take over the world. Rather us than ants or rats, don't you think? I might even get a butler. Mmmmm, there's a thought. xx 🐼😆😆🐼

29ᵗʰ November 2021, continued …

Hi, all. Magical Duke here 😆🐼. Just sticking with Brock, I think. Found an exquisite branch, one of my better ones. Loads of messages on it; plenty of peemails on it; some very important information about safeguarding our patch, which of course is my concern. Ma bought me a Moreno glass clown she thought I would like, as clowning around is my forte. Charity shop, I would bet, but I pretended to be grateful for it—what good it is to me, no idea ☹.

Met a very handsome (nearly as good looking as me) Romanian dog. Had to rack my brain for the bit of Romanian I know, but could only let him sniff my bum. I returned the compliment; well, it's expected, isn't it? Did wipe my nose amongst the leaves. Then bumped into one of my favourite girls, Willow the Westie, who I got pulled away sharpish from when her ma said she was on heat. Lucky girl, I thought; at least somebody is warm 😂😂😊. I can't do anything about, it so what's the problem? Hope everyone is keeping warm too 😂😊😊.

2ⁿᵈ December 2021

Well, guys, had real Swansgate moment this morning. Ma and I doing river walk, but look what was blocking our right of way 😟. The biggest monster, meanest swan ever sighted. There was a smoking lady. Not really seen one before; thought dragon lady, but Ma said, "Don't be rude." She was having a cigarette like they did in the old days. She was standing in her doorway, and she very kindly told us that he was a very dangerous swan and nasty. I barked and threatened him, and cheek of it, it was he gave me a stern swan stare of dismissal and disdain and hissed at us. So pulled myself to full height and with one parting shot told him I was a Magical Duke and a super-Sealyham terrier to boot and sauntered off down a side road and avoided dumb creature, dragging Ma along. Although apparently the lady who lives there feeds him. You should see the state of the path 😖. I prefer vultures circling me, or kites, as Ma calls them (have to humour her sometimes). At least they don't block my way.

The rest of the walk was great saw Debbie, our post lady, on the way going, so treats after I performed my high five my leg going up and down like a piston. Then later on, met the other Debbie—yes two posties called Debbie—so more leg action and more treats. Unbelievable luck; met first Debbie on our way back, so got even more treats. I love our post ladies. Spot 'em a mile off in their red jackets. Sooo not an unprofitable day treat-wise. Keep warm; Brock signing off 😊😊😊.

10ᵗʰ December 2021

Fulfilled one of my dreams to be a post dog today (it's my thing; anybody posting anything or delivering anything I have to lie down and watch; mmmmm, fascinating). Xmas card deliveries. Yahoo! Well, off we charged. Did about three and that was it. Uhmmp. Told I take too long, as I wait outside the houses for the door to open. Well, you never know; might get a chance to nosy in, Ma's cross, as she's on the other end of the lead. (I have to have her on the short lead to keep her in control; she gets so excited sometimes.) Anyway that was the end of that.

Walking along later and a suspicious-looking man (I thought he was a dog snatcher or a drug dealer) hanging around the park entrance asked Ma what sort of dog I was. I felt my lead shorten and she said he's (that's me, Magical Duke Brock super-Sealy) a mongrel. Ohhhh 😟, how rude. Then followed it up by "He's quite old now and castrated"—medical confidentiality gone to pot yet again I have nothing against mongrels, salt of the earth, but really 😟. Anyway, she had the good grace to apologise to me and explain why. Really, lawks alive, I am the neighbourhood watchdog. I know the dangers for us faithful companions, so pretty worn out. Hope you guys have a super weekend and stay safe ♡   😊😊😊.

11ᵗʰ December 2021

This is me last night pretending to be a lapdog 😹🤡. I smothered Ma, but she loved it. This morning, Sunday disaster. I was on the back of the settee, neighbourhood watch duties, giving a warning, rousing tirade, when I suddenly landed on the bay windowsill in the middle of the plants. Soil and leaves flying. *I was pushed.* Yes, can you believe it? Ma did it; she was on the phone and couldn't hear. Pushed my bum—almost a slap! I did threaten her I would be in my rights to report her; plenty of people I could report her to. Don't forget, I'm also on the committee for abolishing aliens and actually hold many important positions, and my name, *Magical Duke*—Royal, you see, as well. I scrambled back up, hoping nobody was passing by. They would have had a great view of my third eye, if you get the drift🤣. So embarrassing. She won't do that again; in a hurry too much mess.

Acted postdog again; xmas card deliveries. Now that's done, looking forward to a rousing evening of disruption to television watching 😧. Strange how it's always a good time for games signing of the Brockster by royal appointment😆. Must get some souvenir mugs made and make some bone money 😼🤡🤡🤡.

15ᵗʰ December 2021

Hi, guys. Well, not blowing my own trumpet but had a big breakthrough yesterday. Went to see sad Mollie. She is pining, still missing Edie, her Scottie friend; not eating and wandering around lost, looking for Edie. Had no luck last week; exhausted my clowning🤡 skills. Second attempt yesterday—gave her lots of mouth kisses and licks. Her tail wagging was a good sign. That night she had her first proper dinner since she lost poor Edie. Soooo I am now a qualified grief counsellor. My fees are very reasonable; a bull's larynx will do, available from our Huntingdon Road pet shop. Bag of tripe an option.

Today I met a doodle dog wearing a Wellington boot 😳. Very smart; he'd cut his paw. Only been in Thrapston a week, so I introduced myself to him. It did take quite a while what with all my titles and qualifications, but he was patient. Then Ma met two of the girls 😹 —ladies, really; fully grown up!—from the surgery where she worked, so that was a boring few minutes for me, as I was being ignored. Commando crawling had no effect. Rude, I thought, so I joined in giving my version of my walk so far. That was rude, Ma said. Ah well, can't win. I am now fetching the post in for her as long as I can give the envelopes a quick shake. I expect pocket money for this

Ma wants her phone back now 🙁 just as my ideas were flowing. Have a good Thursday. xx🤡🤡🤡

17ᵗʰ December 2021

Now, guys, you tell me that this is not debris from a spaceship. See, I know they are around. I gathered intelligence from it to pass on, and I will leave a peemail at my secret dead letter dropoff.

Then 👀 I saw an orange puppy. I really thought that's not right. On closer inspection, he turned out to be a baby whippet in an orange jumper, second day out. So I stood very still, as he was a bit wary—probably bowled over by how debonair I am. As soon as he wanted to play, I was on the ball and had a baby play. His ma was lovely and smelt of sausages right up my street; she had pocket load of these treats 😔. Sadly, didn't get a sample. And then sausage lady and orange baby whippet parted company with us. See, you all thought I was a bull in a china shop, as Ma calls me, but I can be gentle. It's a bit of an ask but can be done.

Last night had late walk in the dark and saw these lights coming towards me. Lawks alive, my heart sank: aliens—never far from my mind. Turned out to be a dog with xmas lights around his neck 😟😂🤣. Nearly forgot: saw a hairy rat up the hairy rat tree as well. Thought they were extinct, as only ever saw one ages ago. Very misty morning; sharp lookout for the living dead crawling, shuffling from the trees into horse paddocks. (Read about them till Ma whipped the book away, saying I have an overactive imagination without any help). Beware, be careful 😄😀😀😀😏.

19ᵗʰ December 2021

Well, guys, what a day. This morning walking up the road, minding my own business for a change, when suddenly really near me one of those red kite/vulture things swooped down in the road, followed by millions. OK, Ma—I am being supervised here—a flock of seagulls screeching, all after the kite/vulture thing, trying to steal his roadkill, even I thought that was unfair. It seems to have been a chariot day. Met two nice ladies who made big fuss of me. I would have liked a ride but wasn't offered one. Then met the two little white guys, one in her own chariot as had bad leg, which is better now, but prefers to be pushed around; she's not daft 😀.

For Miss Ziggy Stardust, our baby tortoise (the one I'm not supposed to know about 😁 Ma's frightened I will think she's a crusty pork pie), it was bath day. Before she went in her bath, I peeped and saw Ma get a tissue and wipe her little tail 😬😱. How gross is that? I know, she helps me sometimes, but never seen her do it for Miss Ziggy Stardust, high and mighty Miss Scaly Legs. Lawks alive. I watched closely, making sure Ma sterilised her hands. Don't need cross infection from a reptile 😱. Just think; if I grew a shell on my back, at least I could join the circus 🎪 then. Resting my paws now; time for a 🛏 signing off. xx

24th December 2021

Well, happy Xmas and happy New Year. Thank you for my Xmas cards I loved them bought them from our letterbox unchewed 😅. Today I acted as GPO escort dog and walked beside our lovely postie Debbie, who gives me treats. I trotted right by the side of her cart tossing my head, looking very official, keeping her and her post safe (neighbourhood watchdog duty); then we parted ways. Back to sniffing peemails—me, not Debbie😗.

Yesterday I nearly got Ma a turkey. Met a friend who was repacking her trolley, and there on the floor, a white cardboard box with a turkey 🦃 inside. Made an ungainly dive for it—lawks alive, I was sooo close—but Ma twigged, and I got pulled away. Met the pug boys and had a sniff and greeting this morning. Going past the graveyard in the mist was scary; not for me, you understand. I have been around the house looking for my pressies, and I don't think Ma was able to get me my own private pooh bin☹.

Our lovely neighbour Angela just been over with lovely flowers for Ma *and* pressies for Miss Ziggy Stardust (the secret tortoise I'm not supposed to know about) and me. Ma making us wait until tomorrow. I am getting even more excited now. Happy Xmas. Stay safe. I am having a mask made for me so I can cover my schnozzle in busy public places so I won't catch Covid 😅😷😷.

1ˢᵗ January 2022

Hi, new year days. Well, I didn't take any notice of the fireworks. Ma was very glad; OK, last year, but just a baby. On our walk I noticed spent rockets about on the ground. Mmmm, just wondering—do they have miniature aliens out there, so small you can hardly see them? It's a thought. I know, Ma says I'm exaggerating all the time, but who knows? She said they were just dead fireworks, but I have super-Sealy powers, so everyone be vigilant.

Met a "Romanian rescue dog" 😜, another breed I've never heard of, like the teacup dogs. He had very long legs, and he left a peemail right up high on this car door. Respect; I can only reach tyres. Well, Ma's in the kitchen I can hear my bowl getting a bit of kibble with my chicken and rice. I will be barking in Cantonese soon. Happy New Year to you all. Love and licks, Brock xx 🐶🐶

8ᵗʰ January 2022

Well, went visiting my recently bereaved pal Mollie, whose Ma is desperate to rehome an older Scottie to keep her company. Well, I licked her face; she likes that. Although she's very old, she even tried to play with me today before she crashed out in a very ungainly pose, which I chose to ignore. Off I went in search of a toy and found a great one—the cat's bowl—so I ran around like mad and only dropped it when Ma yelled, "Cheese!" Fair exchange; I'm not daft 😵‍💫🐶. So I'm hoping my grief counselling worked, and she ate her food. I get my certificate after the third counselling session 🐶🐶🐶.

9th January 2022

Hi there. I have found space debris 👽. I just knew it; those spent rockets on the path at New Year's, and now this. I had a really good cautious examination. You can't be too careful; might still be radioactive. Ma hummphed and told me to hurry up and that it was the top of an incinerator bin. Well, poor soul, she's so gullible. I really have to look out for her. I went along with the bin lid story so as not to frighten her, but I will be watching and have reported it to my superiors—hard to think that super-Sealies have superiors, but we are all answerable to higher powers.

Had lots of feline sightings which I had to sort out on my walk; problematical, as I need to concentrate on my peemails. I was recognised as a Sealy this morning by a lovely lady. Usually it's "Is he a westie or westie cross?" 🙄 No, I am me in my own right as a proud Sealyham—clown 🤡 of the terrier group. Takes skills to be funny. Well, off for last smaller walk, as did the long one this morning. See how filthy I can get my undercarriage; bit of commando crawling might do the trick 😂😂😃😃.

11th January 2022

Poor moles; each molehill looked like a mini Everest. Thick white frost on top. Wonder if they have to wear thermal mittens on their shovelly paws. Got to report a sighting of hairy grey rat running up its tree; excited, as might catch it another day.

Got real black tongue envy; my mate from Yugoslavia is a Chow cross and has a large black tongue. Asked Ma if she would dye mine. That was a no goer. She told me to own my big long pink tongue and be proud of it, no matter where it's been or going to be 😋😝 in the future. Met some sheepdogs—? Didn't look at all like the sheep I've seen in the market; they are mostly white and woolly.

Loved the thick frost, rolling around in it, eating it, commando crawling. Yes, it was a very slow walk. Met the little border terrier (there again I don't get the names they call these breeds—does she need a visa or passport? I'm just going to roll with it), and our ma's were talking—something about classes. Hmmmmph; Ma is trying to get me into classes, I think. Shudder to think why. I can text in English obviously; do I make any mistakes? Not many, so—? We'll have to see. If I don't like it, I can always get expelled 😃😂.

Found a rigid dead glove in the frost. Allowed to take it on my walk and no further. My collection has to end. Ma has had enough. My museum of corpses has been unceremoniously chucked out. so will have to look for something else now. Hope you all have a great weekend. 🐶🐶🐶 sloppy licks

20th January 2022

Wombling duties; lovely walk this morning. Very frosty—lovely to commando crawl through. Lots of smells on town walk: deer, rabbit, badgers, and fox, but you guessed it: no fox pooh 🐶 and me fresh from grooming, clean as a whistle, thwarted again in my quest for elusive fox pooh, so hmmmp; really quite white still 😵.

Lawks alive, last night I was lounging on our bed. Ma was in the computer room and spare bedroom (really, delusions of grandeur; bless her), and then I heard a loud explosion. I shot off the bed and flew in to see what had happened 😵🙄🥴. "Sorry," she said, "it was only me sneezing." Well, I really thought she had blown up; expected to see her splattered all over the walls. It's just as frightening as when she's singing: dreadful noise. Getting used to it now, but thought I was losing her the first time; sounded as though she was in her death throes. I really have a lot to put up with, on top of which I heard whispers of a wedding that I'm not invited to next month. Dreading to see what she's going to do with me for four or five days—home alone? 🙄🥴 That I could cope with, but that won't wash, so will wait and see. Licks to all 👅👅🐶🐶.

23rd January 2022

Morning; happy Sunday. Good walk this morning. Met four-month-old English bull terrier. She was great fun; we had good wrestle and had to be separated, or we would have gone forever. Sadly, her Ma said a lot of people cross the road to avoid them because of the breed she is 😵. She's gorgeous—what a Roman nose—but my schnozzle itself is bigger 🐶.

The walk got better. I found a dead bobble hat that was definitely a collectable piece, but no. I was told to leave it on the hedge in case owner found it. Lawks alive; deprived of a really good find. Later on found dead glove; boring. But here comes the best ever: a huge beef crisp bag, empty. Ma thought I knew better; got nearly home and couldn't wait any longer. One good shake and Eureka, out they tumbled: two whole crisps and lots of crumbs. Of course I let Ma carry the empty bag the rest of the way home back to our bin; didn't interest me anymore, although it did still smell good. So she became my Womble helper. Thrilled she was not 🙄🥴🐶🐶👅👅. Licks to you all.

26th January 2022

The other day I had the most worrying experience. Four small people were locked in a cage in their garden; Ma called it a trampoline, but I think it's a cage. you could see them quite clearly. They were jumping up and down, higher and higher trying to escape, shouting loudly. I just stood rooted to the spot. Wanted Ma to call the police I watched for ages and they were still trapped. Ma assured me it was just a game. Ummph; have my doubts, but this morning the cage was empty, so they must have jumped over the top and escaped.

Had great games this morning with young Alsatian girl and Labs and retriever lad about my age. Ma very pleased with me and my approach to cats now. I control Sealy urge to yell at the top of my voice. Still have to give my super-Sealy killer frown, but hey. Must admit, though: yesterday I did have a puppy relapse. While Ma was in the bathroom, I stole one of her boots and stripped the lining out. Whoa, the fuss. Still looks OK from the outside. Shucks then of course there was the famous ham and coleslaw baguette snatch. Cor, I was soo fast. There it was on the plate on Ma's knee, then gone.😂😂😂🤡.

I really missed walking with the baby and her pushchair today. And there is no sign of Ma's baby I asked her to get for me. Maybe she will just get a pushchair that I can walk with; maybe put Miss Ziggy Stardust in it (will find a right time to tell Ma she's not really a secret). Have a happy sunny day 👅👅🤡🤡🤡🤡.

4th February 2022

Happy Saturday to you all. You might think I am in the jungle. Ummph; may as well be. Ferns blocking my view of workmen doing a drive opposite, and I do like to supervise. I can see that new kid on the block—a cat, yes, a cat. It taunts me; came in my garden. Can you imagine? Super-Sealy killer frown was in full force, but think it's an alien cat with a protective shield around it. Be better if it had an invisible cloak over it, and I could get some peace. No respect for neighbourhood super-Sealy watchdog, which is my proud position and duty to our close. Bid you bye, as must take Ma out for her exercise and hope she behaves. Lick lick 👅👅🤡🤡.

7th February 2022

Hi, guys, look what I found: big empty milk container. People laughed at me rude! Carried it right to the front door where—you guessed it—it was unceremoniously dumped in our bin. Lawks alive. I call that very hard to accept, but there you go. Early on in the walk, a man watched me all the way down the road and then said he hadn't seen a Sealy for ages, and I was the second in two weeks. He is thinking of getting one as always wanted one. I backed away just in case. Worryingly he had smoke coming from his cupped hand 😨. I thought he might burst into flames, but Ma told me to pull myself together; it was only a cigarette.

Off we waddled and wow: spotted a round flat shiny shape on the ground next to a dustbin. Well, that went straight in the mouth, and I was having a good chew on it. Ma nearly had a fit; dived on me, assaulted me, thrust her hand in my mouth. In the end I swapped it for a gravy biscuit; mmmm. It was a can lid. Luckily didn't cut my mouth.

Real find of all I've ever had was a pushchair, just pushed in by a bush. You all know I have pushchair envy. *No*. Of course I was heartbroken. I pleaded with Ma, promised her a ride and I could pull her along like a chariot. *No*. Well, could she push me along? *No*. So that was when I had to content myself with empty milk container.

Ma then went out later to come back smelling of Alsatians. Got very excited. She had been to River's house. She told me how beautiful Riv was and her four other Alsatian pals. I think she even kissed Ma, 'cos I smelt her up near her neck. Ma said she would make a very suitable girlfriend for me; I like 'em big😆. Wonder what goodies are lying around for me to collect tomorrow. Paws crossed. Have another plead about the pushchair, but bet she won't go that way. Aren't ma's spoilsports sometimes? 😫👅👅🐶🐶

8ᵗʰ February 2022

Hi, guys; the Brockster here. Walking Ma this morning, I thought I would have fun and pretend I'm a one-tusked elephant. Kinda awkward, so that didn't last long. Afternoon—well thereby hangs a tail (😆🐶). See what I did there? 🤣 What a card. Took Ma to dog training classes 😃. Embarrassing. Lawks alive; first she got lost. She knocked on a house door, and apparently we had been yards away. When she did three-point turn, closed my eyes, as big ditch each side of lane. Arrived ten minutes late.

Ma embarrassed me; we had to walk forward and then backwards😆🤣. Ma nearly landed on her backside. Lots of padding there, so she would have been all right. Then there was a chicken lady next to us who kept feeding her dog—and so I'm straight in there in front, doing high fives, and it worked. Lots of sitting by Ma's left heel, lying down, and walking around the other guys who stood in a ring. Teacher gave Ma a big smelly biscuit to hold at my nose level and take me around to heel. She looked like Quasimodo. I had to laugh; bet she wished I had long legs. At the end she was supposed to reward me, and I was overcome with greed urge and took the whole biscuit. Ma was told only tiny bit at a time. Well, she knew that, but I was in super-Sealy mode; she didn't stand a chance. I really hope she improves by next week. I will get her to practice. At least she wasn't expelled. First time; plenty of time for that to happen.

Resting my paws now; will keep you posted 👅👅🐶🐶. I kept looking at the jumps and the poles you weave through. I'll make short work of them— plow right through them when I am allowed. Sooo school has started.

14ᵗʰ February 2022

Hey, all—wicked Wednesday. Can't wait to get out of this infernal place my second visit. Well, after slipping my collar three times and having a good trot around all the other dogs, well, only polite, isn't it? Recaptured, and if I barked, a squirt of water in my face by teacher. How rude is that 😳. Not at all woke—whatever that means. Disgraceful really.

Tried to get me to jump over poles. *What?* I'm not a horse. In fact, I completely disintegrated one; poles and struts flying in all directions😆😂🐶. Then there was a tunnel thing like aunty Pat has for her cat 😼. Lawks alive, I'm certainly not one of those; how degrading. Walking to heel I got praised for; I only did it because Ma had a treat in her hand. Sit, and stay, and come, piece of ——. I'd practised that at home. Ma did say to bossy lady teacher, "Could we have settees in here and Brock will jump on them, no problem?" No luck there. As for weaving through the poles, not even offered the chance. Just as well. I already had a demolition plan in place.

Must say it's boring walking around to heel. At one point I put my paw down and had a hissy-fit tantrum; that stopped them 😂🤭. I then behaved for a while. Sooo I did get some praise at some points. I do not have to wear school uniform next week, which is just a collar. I can also be allowed to wear my harness. Made Ma tear up my university application form. Don't want to go anymore. *I hate school.* Ma just made me say teacher really nice; well, I beg to differ🐶🐶🐶🐾🐾.

20ᵗʰ February 2022

Hey, guys, guess what Ma bought me from her shopping expedition today? My very own Six Nations rugby ball; love it. This morning met little lady French bulldog. She had what looked like a black tyre around her neck 😳; very alarming. Wanted to report to the authorities. I've seen pictures of people with them around their necks, and nasty people set fire 🔥 to them. Ma told me to stop being an alarmist, that I too had a blue one after my demasculating op done. Forgotten that; try to put that memory in a black box in my mind.

Just around the corner saw a trio of Chinese crested dogs 😂. They pranced past, hair flying on head, tails, and feet. Don't speak Chinese yet—on my to-do list—so just gave a cheeky wink which was answered by a curled lip. Ah well. Going out soon in storm Franklin. It's getting worse; will lash Ma to my harness and hope she doesn't blow over. Her size sevens should keep her grounded. Uh-uh; just got told not to be personal. Stay safe, everyone 🐶🐶🐾🐾🐾.

27ᵗʰ February 2022

Hi, there. I was whacked out after my prison sentence—oh, OK; Ma looking over my shoulder—my luxury kennel stay. Just between us, I really enjoyed Denford Edge Kennels. Lots of dogs, and the girls kind, but not letting Ma know, as she's feeling guilty. Shame to spoil that 😵‍💫🤡. Sleep deprivation was the only drawback; the snoring and noisy dream sounds, and occasionally one of my fellow inmates would yelp out loud. Nightmares, I assume. Takes a lot to bring super-Sealies down. I might only be sixteen months old, but I am a fast learner. You have to be to keep up with all the different languages. I have to learn lots of Romanian, as there are a lot of immigrants in town. Definitely refuse to learn cat language; put my paw down there.

Lovely to be home again, though. Back checking all the peemails today, then found a really dangerous stick full of thorns, so that was confiscated 😵. I even missed Miss Ziggy Stardust moaning away about how noisy I am. Had lain in this morning until 9.15 on our bed. Ma was up earlier 😂🤣🤡, so crawled into her spot of the bed. Quite small, even though king-size bed. I take up most of it😂🤣🤡🤡🤡🫵🫵🫵.

27ᵗʰ February 2022, continued ...

Well, here I am. Been bathed, brushed, and combed and trimmed. I absolutely got beside myself when Ma said the name *Susie*. I kept watch for her car. She takes me, and Ma collects me. I love Susie.

Anyway, eventful afternoon walk, *very*. Chancery Lane pavements very narrow, but still managed to gamble with a poo boy cockapoo. I think the ma's were chatting away when I spotted yet another poo boy across the road. I dived, dragging Ma sideways. Down she went—she blames me 😳. Was I the one that got my size sevens in a twist? No; landed on her side—*so* embarrassing. Didn't know where to look as two ladies hauled her to her feet, blood pouring through her jeans from knees—oh my. People all concerned, but Ma told me she was so padded up with clothes, it really only hurt her pride. You know, "Pride comes before a fall." Anyway, I know Ma; tough old bird. Oops, got a warning look from Ma. She said that was disrespectful. She has survived many a super-Sealy assault. I must remember, I am a very strong boy.

Must just say met a lovely American bulldog girl, Lana. Younger than me. She taught me some American words too. Signing off, as my time on Ma's phone is up 🐶🐶😃😃.

PS: Ma said to add she is fine, thank you, and really looking forward to our next walk 😂😃😃🐶🐶.

1 March 2022

Well, hi there. Lovely day. Firstly, I haven't a report about school, as I didn't go 😀. Had serious talk with Ma. She hated school, so I had a sympathetic ear. We both decided that I didn't enjoy or want to jump fences; said before, not a horse. Certainly didn't want to weave through poles—what's that all about?—and as for that tunnel thing, that's for cats. I know, as Ma's friend has one for her cat, which I might say I never met: she gets locked in a bedroom as if I was a savage 😳. Probably for the best as I would love a good chase.

Next year I am going to text Mr Cruft, who holds the shows, as my entrepenpaw side of me has got to thinking of a new event: sofa leaping. I am bound to excel in that; I literally fly from one end of the room to the other end, sofas at both ends. Only landed on the windowsill once; plants all over the place. I actually am so fast my paws get carpet burns😃.

Just a thought here: am I the only one who wonders about these doodle dogs? They are around every corner. Is there going to be a coup, doodles v pure breeds? We truly are a rare breed. Guys, if Ma hadn't demasculated me, I would willingly father many Sealies a day. I would make it my aim in life; can't think of a better occupation. Ah, well—never know. Have to rely on the studs to keep us thriving. Have a happy day 🐶🐶😃😃.

4th March 2022

Hi, guys. Well, yesterday I had two lovely ladies visit me, Dani and Emma from Rectory Farm, with a view for me to have a regular playday in their paddock with lots of companions. Well, I put on my best licky loving behaviour, although couldn't help stealing one of their boots, but brought it in to them undamaged—that took self-control. Today Ma took me through town, and it was farmers' market day. Don't think she'll do that again. Mmmmmm, the smells. My big black schnozzle was glued to the stalls, all of them.

Met some nice pals on the way home. I wanted a stick so I did a Houdini and Magical Duke. I lived up to my title; out of my harness—freeee. I was good; didn't run away, and soon, on way back, whoa: who was coming down my road? My nemesis lanky-legged spotty boy Dalmatian 😕.

Ma asked the man if I could come and say hello 😳😳😳😃. What was she thinking? We'd be best buddies after a nose sniff? I stalked up to him and sniffed noses; then I let out a super-Sealy roar louder than a lion. I get on with most other dudes, but no way. I think he's got a disease—all those spots. Of course I embarrassed Ma, but hey, I will give her a sloppy kiss, and it will all be sweet. Have a great weekend 🐶🐶😃😃.

8th March 2022

Well, I loved my playday at Rectory Farm and can't wait till next week. Emma came to pick me up, and I got really excited and off in the van we went. Dani sent Ma video to show I was fine. I ran and ran and ran—wheeee; love those girls. When Emma brought me home, I am afraid couldn't help myself but didn't want to go in. I wriggled trying to get back to the van. Emma had to bring me into the kitchen. Dani and Emma both said I was a good boy and fitted in straight away. I love Rectory Farm playdays; roll on next Tuesday 🐶🐶😃😃.

14th March 2022

Well, new phone sorted. I'm wearing paw mittens, as Ma doesn't want new phone scratched, and screen saver on its way. Ma said guy in the shop said if dog drool got on the sim, that could have made our phone go strange. *How rude was that?* So of course we all know who is getting the blame: moi😆. It was certainly possessed; used to do things on its own and kept freezing all the time.

Dreadful teatime. My nemesis, the devil-spotted creature, went passed my house twice. Well, I nearly propelled myself through the window and got told off just for voicing my opinion. Also, Ma said I had got to stop swearing, as it doesn't make me look any bigger. I know that, but boy, makes me feel better. My pocket money is being reduced so I can use this phone, which is a liberty, and I had to promise not to carry it around in my mouth. Well, I've grown up a bit since those days. Signing off now, as hate these mittens.😃

14th March 2022, continued …

Wheeee. HI, all. Playschool day. Had lovely, lovely morning at Dani and Emma's at their paddock. Still waiting for my red cape so I look the part of super-Sealy Magical Duke Brock. I nearly took off this morning. I am going to practice levitation; sure that would help.

Weird house we live in. Heard Ma muttering away about creeping rugs🐶. I've heard of flying carpets, but ours must be poor quality if they can only manage to creep. Fright of my life this afternoon. Ma got this contraption from a cupboard and put water in it. Well, it sounded possessed, spitting and hissing, and she was putting it on her clothes (she's not very domesticated), so it was quite a rare sighting. Thought my wavy hair was going to be next, so casually wandered off. Hope you all have had a good day 😃😃😃.

16th March 2022

Now not happy ☹. No. Objected to being dressed up. Led Ma a merry dance but let her get her way. Pouring with rain and wanted my walk, sooo didn't meet anybody else; little wonder. Glad really, as Ma started what she calls singing "The Day that the Rains Came Down". Heard better from that dreadful cat thing over the road; would have been mortified if she had been overheard. Saw a hairy rat jumping through the trees.

I was concerned about the poor blind shovel-fisted mole things. Asked Ma would they drown—pouring rain on their mole hills; didn't get an answer. Sooo my Magical Duke side of me kicked in, and I weaved a protection spell, but it could only be cast if I had peed on every one, so all the mole hills got even wetter, but it was magic pee⚡ so that was fine, my good deed for the day.

I had to laugh. Miss Ziggy Stardust muttered that she'd done a whoopsy on her feeding slate, so Miss 'sun shines out of her shell' is not perfect 😂. Dinner time now, so this damp dog will enjoy chicken and kibble 🐶🐶🐶.

17th March 2022

Well, what a lovely day. I've had morning walk, and Debbie postie back. Made a beeline for her. Sat there looking like a depraved windup dog, my right leg pumping up and down in high fives. Really earned my treat; in fact, got two.

Next funny thing was by the lakes a lady walking her two little people and swinging a paper bag from her hand, when a passing golden retriever casually walked past and, fast as you like, snatched the bag of bread for the ducks from her hand. The owner was mortified. Ma was laughing, and I had bread envy. So the ducks didn't get as much as they had hoped for. I met a really handsome doodle retriever ma and black poodle pa. He was only young but so tall; beautiful black coat. Looked just like a standard poodle but heavier built. Had a bit of fun with him and then ever onwards.

This afternoon went down to the horses' paddocks, and a stray chucky hen had strayed from her field onto the path. Well, my first close encounter with one. She came clucking right up to me. Could feel Ma holding on for dear life. Ohhhh, I was magnificent. Down on my haunches, neck down and straight out, creeping slowly forward. Silly thing didn't seem aware of the mighty hunter nearly nose to beak. I sprang forward, but of course Ma held tight, and the chuck went squawking off, feathers flying. There went my chicken dinner; very disappointing outcome, but at least I proved myself to Ma as well, as I really think I would have done a mischief to that chuck. At least I haven't got blood on my paws so not in the doghouse😀😀.

26th March 2022

Well, yesterday a very truck-orientated day. First was a big van delivering rolls of tripe at the pet shop. Ooooh, I just followed my big black schnozzle. The doors were wide open. In I went well— my front half. Luckily the driver thought it was very funny 😀. Shame I couldn't tuck a tripe roll under my armpit and smuggle it off the van, but Ma's beady eye (she's only got one beady, as the other has to have cataract done) was watching my every move. She warned me about dog jail; not like my luxury kennel I had before, so decided to stay on the straight and narrow for now. Might turn to a life of crime later. Ummm; see how it goes.

Then further down the road what did I see but a very large lorry with the cab door *open*. Well, before you could say lawks alive, the driver said good day and invited me in (he wasn't Australian, by the way). Well, must say it was quite a struggle up very high steps. I was very impressed with all the controls. Could I possibly retrain from a super-Sealy clown😀 with special controls fitted in the cab and become a lorry driver? Ma said forget that right away and told me that I shouldn't try and climb into anything with an open door. Must say I do do that, and I take sweets—well, treats—from strangers too. Suppose not a good idea, as Ma said that there are bad people out there, and she could not be without me. I know I am a big help to her. As I have my Master's in Sealy clownshipness, thinking of doing professor exams. And I would be even more qualified to join the circus; just imagine a clown 😀 with a big black nose instead of a red one 😂😄. Food for thought and on that line of thought, stopping now as tuna and kibble dinner coming up. Have a lovely weekend. I have sent a big bone to my doggy Ma for Mother's Day. (That's a lie, but I am thinking of her😋.)

26th March 2022, continued ...

Lovely walk by the lakes 😍met a lovely cockajack puppy girl. She used language I couldn't understand, but Ma said it was Jordie, whichever country that is. Quite honestly, I've not got enough brain room left, as it's full of refugee dogs language who I chat to. Must say not bragging; well, would I? But know about four different languages😊, although must admit English is not so strong. Difficulty coping with *No, Come here, Drop that*—mundane things like that.

Two strange things, met a border terrier whose ma said she wasn't well; had a phantom pregnancy. Oooh 👻how spooky was that? See, ghosts do exist, and as I believe, aliens do too. Next thing was quite alarming: a man walking along with a small person growing out of his shoulders. Well, that's just wrong. I just stared; Ma said not to be rude. I expressed my views, yipping and yowling away, and was assured all normal; it was called giving a piggyback. Humans have really strange habits. What would you think if I walked around with a puppy on my shoulders, and where does piggy fit in 🐷? Ah well, more research to do.

Ma's Day today, so my beloved Adrian and Lonnie visited. So excited. I was probably overenthusiastic, but hey. My Sealy ma lives in Essex; think she's the original "Essex Girl", but licks and Sealy beardy kisses to her. Hope all ma's had a lovely day ♡ 😊.

31st March 2022

Well, be still, my beating heart 😲. Ma and I were on our morning patrol checking all was safe and updating my peemails when I saw the big van approach and park. And lawks alive, who should step out but Dani one of my playday supervisors? Well, I was all over her like a rash, *but* she wasn't taking me; it was another dog. Well, I was rooted to the spot, paddock envy oozing out of my very being. Ma eventually got me moving again.

We overslept this morning, and Ma hadn't even had her cuppa. Earlier we had met another mate of mine, Teddy the Pomeranian—not I might add, named after a teacup or any other kitchen object. We had a little dash about. This town is riddled with Poms. Must keep a watchful Sealy eye 👁 on the situation; could be a coup about to happen. His ma said hi to my ma and then said, "Oh, this is the unusual dog, isn't it?" (plainly forgetting what breed I was), but I'll take that as a compliment—beggars can't be choosers, as the saying goes.

Well, Ma had an official letter, which I didn't shred before she got it, and she said we needn't worry about affording my treats and pocket money. The government had given her a pension rise. I got so excited until she told me 25p a week. Well, that won't even buy me a chew. Think I will have to take the situation in my Sealy paws. I will have to get a job as a guard dog; that would be a help. I am learning to snarl and froth at the mouth and have asked Ma for a collar with big spikes on it to get the message across. Stay warm 😊😊. 😠 My work expression 😁.

2nd April 2022

Sunbathing but in deep doo-doo. Ma was cutting honeysuckle hedge and brushing up when she suddenly noticed soil all over the patio 😳. Well, I was only helping her, for goodness' sake. Saw this twig sticking out of a pot and ran off with it. Did I know it was her baby climbing jasmine? *No*, I am not a blooming gardener. Had noticed it had been fenced off, which of course drew my attention. The big unveiling only happened this morning because I hadn't bothered with it 🐷.

It's now been put behind a little fence. Admittedly I can't resist a stick and of course never saw the green leaves. That's the last time Ma gets my help gardening; her loss. 🐨

3ʳᵈ April 2022

There I was last night curled up next to Ma watching *Peaky Blinders*. They were shooting eyes out, blowing people up, the usual (Ma said not to make this a spoiler as people might not have seen it yet), but pans into Tommy (Ma's fave) lying on the grass. Then most frightening, menacing thing happened: ginormous black crows walking around Tommy. *Well*, enough is enough; I thought a step too far. Off the settee, wide awake, and flung myself at those revolting crows, and they disappeared. I went around the side of the picture box, but not a sign, so back onto the settee. Job done, and then lying down, one 👁 open just in case. See, I haven't done a spoiler. Happy Monday 🐨🐨🐨.

5ᵗʰ April 2022

Well, watching my favourite programme: dogs behaving very badly, as it makes me look good😆 —although I did get told off for shouting encouraging tips to them. Still clean from my spa day yesterday, but I could see Ma grimace, a look of pain on her face, every time I did my commando walking on the pavement. Tomorrow my chances improve. Paddock playday: bound to find a bit of muck to roll in, even the elusive fox poo. I asked Ma to put the picture of me on, posing looking out of the window wistfully, as I even impressed myself 🐨😆😂.

9th April 2022

Hey, guys, guess what I acquired on yesterday's walk—a lovely fox toy, *No*, didn't steal it from any little people. Given it by a man from a pile of free toys. I carried it all the way home. Crossing the park very worried (I am an anxious Sealy diagnosed). I saw lovely lady who looks after little people, and she was behind bars with her little people, and they were going down slides and having fun. So wanted to go in and join in, but Ma said forbidden, and the bars and fence were to keep me out. Rude, I thought, so just had to stick my nose through the bars, leaving Foxy (made that name up; ingenious, isn't it?) with Ma. Didn't trust those little people; might try and steal Foxy away from me. They can be devious.

Later Adrian, Ma's son, came over. Joy, joy, lawks alive, I was all over him. Love him to bits, so he got a good super-Sealy licking. This morning went through the woods, and there were hairy rats jumping around in the trees. Dash, can't climb trees; might damage my texting paw, and that would be dreadful. Well, off to help Ma gardening 😂😂😺😺. This could be catastrophic.

9th April 2022 (Sealyham meet-up Cambridge and East Anglia)

Well, what a day. Firstly, Auntie Jenny arrived, and I managed to get into her bag and ran off with her glasses. Method in my madness, yup. Ma yells cheese, and there you have it. Drop the glasses; no harm done. Bit of fun, and I won a piece of cheese 😺. Then off we go in the car. They put me in the back 😿. Well, I made such a noise in protest, Aunt J swopped seats, and I got my front seat back. It is my duty to keep an eye on Ma when she gets behind the wheel. After hours and hours—oh, OK; forty-five minutes; just felt longer—Fineshade Wood loomed ahead. Another hour or so before Ma had mastered the ticket machine 😑. Well, it felt like that, and we're off.

Must admit I was overexcited, pulling like a plough horse, but much faster, Ma's arm stretching longer and longer. Met all the Sealies, and some had bought pals along. Had good sniffs at all the important areas as we do. Scrounged some treats. Then Eddie and Buffy and Mr and Mrs E arrived, and we were soon off. Did I walk nicely? *No*. I was in such a hurry. There were lovely, dirty, watery, muddy parts by the roadside. Was I allowed in? No. I came the closest I have ever come in my short life to the elusive (to me anyway) fox poo, but before I could get to it, somebody kicked it off the path into a ditch 😕, so missed my chance to become of age—baptism by fox poo.

Lovely, sunny day. Really enjoyed it, and I tried not to be rude. Whacked out now; don't need afternoon walk. Ma secretly happy, as she hopes her arm will shrink back to its normal length soon. Got to say I don't pull like that normally. Thank you, Eddie, Buffy, and Mr and Mrs E for organizing it 😺.

12th April 2022

Well, paddock playschool was amazing; no dirt involved though 😬. Butterflies 🦋🦋🦋 —lots about on our afternoon walk. Lady came up and asked Ma if her name was Val. She owned up to it, and then I got the attention, as this lady had heard all about me (not bad things, I hope). Her friend had told her about us. I think I'm going to hire security to keep me safe from mishaps and bad people. Thinking of smuggling in a pit bull or two with spiky collars. Luckily all the people Ma and I meet are lovely, and if I don't get a treat, lots of fuss—oh, OK. Ma has just told me off and told me to keep my paws on the ground and not get carried away so no Papp's ☺. Was rather looking forward to flashbulbs and lots of pics.

At the end of our walk, met my nemesis, long-legged spotty dog. Well, let myself and Ma down. I cussed and snarled, growled, tried to foam at the mouth but didn't succeed, with just a bit of spit coming out; not very impressive. I just can't help myself. My theory is, the spotty creature is highly contagious. And now Ma has taken my mask away. Well, lawks alive, I am open to contamination. Have to go, as Ma has got the sole of her boot to clean; *not to blame* 🤡🤡.

13th April 2022

Well, hi there. I just knew that putting a touch of eau de chien behind my ears would have the desired effect. Have met lots of pals today and newbies, and I have been thoroughly sniffed from head to tail. Lots of interest; I must be very alluring. Saw two corpses today; great. Vultures 🫣 could have been pigeons thinking about it. Good job for Ma that she made me get rid of my museum of corpses. They looked lovely and yuck, though good enough to roll on, which of course I wasn't allowed to do.

Met my Spinone mates. I always get a paw pat on my head, which completely covers my head; friendly lads. Have thought of wearing a crash hat. Save me getting brain damage. Walking along nicely when wowee, lawks alive, Ma made that noise as though she was blowing up. Sneezing, she calls it. Very alarming. I always rush up to her, make sure top of her head is still on; embarrassing too. Big responsibility looking after Ma. She is so clumsy too; trip over a leaf, she would. Hope you all enjoyed your Wednesday 🤡.

15th April 2022

Yesterday saw the most peculiar thing. People on bits of plastic on the river. I was waiting for one to sink; 😵 never happened. They had even chased that frightful dangerous swan 🦢 thing out of the water 😤, putting Ma and me in danger of hissing, wing-flapping creature. No biggie; my super-Sealy killer frown will protect us.

Then met a lovely lady and friend and she petted me and said, "Is he a Schnauzer?" Strewth; bury me bone, and lawks alive. So Ma gave her a brief background about Sealyhams and how rare we are. Still, enjoyed the fuss. Met lots of people and their four-legged friends; had lots of sniffing and little games with them. On the way home saw an abandoned tricycle. I pleaded, "Perleeease, can we take it home and I could learn to ride it?" The first Sealy bike rider (still have yearnings to join a 🎪 circus). Wouldn't leave Ma, though she could be my agent, and the secret Miss Ziggy Stardust who I'm not supposed to know about, could be my publicist. See, I would provide for my family—pay them in Gravy Bones biscuits if that would work 🤭. Of course the trike never came home with me. What's the use of being a striving entrepawneer if you are not allowed to follow your dreams and ideas? Must have words with Ma. collection of rare sticks, corpse museum, and rubbish collection all end by my front door, not forgetting the human clothes collection. Ah well, back to the drawing board. Have a super Easter 🐰🐰🐰😃.

22ⁿᵈ April 2022

Ratgate ... well, mullocky walk this morning. First I was on the cat trail, head down, nose to ground. Then suddenly different smell; mmmmm, interesting. Then to Ma's disgust the biggest ex-rat, big as my head—oh, here she goes 😵. OK, Ma, nearly as big. Even Ma said she'd never seen one that big. Flat as a pancake and headless, right by cemetery railings. Shame not intact; sort of second-hand corpse. Well, such a fine specimen if only I had been allowed to keep my museum of corpses. Pleaded with Ma could we pickle it first. As it was so flat, she could have had it as a throw rat mat. Seen mats like dead tigers and sheepskins, so I know they exist. Umph; bury me bone. Not having any of that. Really. So I had to leave that fine spec lying squashed by the cemetery railings. So sulky Sealy kicked in, commando crawling, lying on my back, kicking my legs in the air, on the grass. Ohh, I made her pay.

At last I saw a cat in the distance and shot up like a rocket and off. Met all sorts of delivery vans, and had to wait if they parked for the drivers to get out and fuss me, and I usually treat them to a commando crawl. Then to cap it all, turned corner to cross over road to come home when that lanky-legged spotted dog, my nemesis, appeared. Well, even I must say I frightened myself, the row I made, and lawks alive, he just danced past, wagging his thin tail. Even that's spottier; swear his spots are spreading. And that stupid grin—ooooofff—infuriates me. Ma said he's a good dog, as he doesn't answer back. Still trying hard to foam at the mouth; that should be scary, coupled with my super-Sealy killer frown 😡😼😃.

24ᵗʰ April 2022

Awwww, bin day today. Off we go, and I was lucky enough to be bin escort dog. I trotted along and lay down when it stopped to ensure no juicy bits of anything dropped out (really, not that fussy). Ma was not amused, as she didn't share my pure enjoyment of the stink rolling in vapours from the lorry. Lawks alive, it was good. Almost as good as corpse smell. Ma had words: asked if I'd rather not collect and press flowers 🙄. Bury me bone and kick me butt, what does she think I am 🤡? Nope, sticking to the most repulsive (to Ma anyway) mashed-up things I can find.

Off for p.m. walk now. Gathered treats off lovely postie this morning; she gave me double, as I high-fived so much Ma said I looked like a Nazi, whatever that is. Searching for hoof trimmings by the paddocks this afternoon. Miss Ziggy Stardust has had her bath (which she pooed in; no manners for all her hoity-toity ways 😂🤣). Hope you have all had a good Monday 🤡.

1ˢᵗ May 2022

Catgate affair. Well, the cheek of it. What a disgusting performance; real challenge to my street cred. Ma and I walking along this morning, I poked my head around into a garden. Lawks alive, bury me bone, and OMG. Hissing, puffed-up black-and-white *giant* cat came leaping out at us (would have been safer on safari!). It lurched out walking sideways, spitting, growling, open-mouthed snarling—well, I let forth best Sealy barks I could do. Ma was pulling me back by my Julius K brassiere as hard as she could, *and* it chased us up the road and round the corner. We must have looked a sight 😳; unbelievable.

This afternoon went to Auntie Pat's. I got a bit bored and was trying to eat her sofa in the dining room; just came over me 🙄; really couldn't help myself. Ma was mortified. Still bored, so jumped on Auntie Pat's chair to apologise; gave her a Sealy kiss. Then the chair came to life, moving up and down. Oh, my sainted mother—whatever next? So had to bark at that. Then I hid behind the laurel hedge in her garden and watched Ma and Auntie Pat looking for me. They were getting quite worried. Then Auntie Pat spotted me 👀. Yes, I'd got stuck; hmmmp. So they hauled me out.

Did redeem myself later and made Ma proud of me 😇. A teeny fifteen-weeks cockapoo came running up to me, jumping all over my head, even sitting on it, and I just stood still as a statue cos I remember I used to do that. Met a chiapoo yesterday—full grown but obviously very small. Think a stepladder must have been involved in that love match 😬. Think poodles are taking over the world. Bank holiday Monday was quite lively; hope you all enjoyed yours 🤡.

4th May 2022

Watergate 🤣😂. Well, I did pester to go out. Just got past the fairy tree and down by the paddocks, and lawks alive, bury me bone, a deluge the heavens opened. But still had to have my smells before they were carried away by the floods. (Should have had my life jacket on in case I too got carried away.) The skies were black; in fact, Ma said it was called a cloudburst, and I certainly didn't need a life jacket.

Had a busy day. While Ma was doing things on the computer, I snuck into the back bedroom, where I am forbidden to go 😇. Liberated one of her long boots and a weeny grey koala bear that had fallen off the windowsill and crept downstairs. As I was being very quiet, Ma came down to check on me. The koala had been decapitated, and I had the insole out of her boot. Well, spoilsport! That was it; boring 😑. And that was when I pestered for a walk. Hmmmp; what comes round goes round. So I got drenched (but so did Ma). My beard will never be the same again; neither will Ma's be 🤣😂🤣. Did you like my joke? *And* the rain has made me all clean again after my successful filthifying attempt in the clean paddocks at playschool yesterday. Hope you had better weather than we did today 🤡♡   .

5th May 2022

Cavegate. Lovely walk yesterday morning by the lake. Evil swans in the distance. Discovered a cave/tunnel hidden in the jungle; couldn't believe how lucky I was. Maybe it's full of troglodytes—scary cave dwellers who steal out in the night to pillage. Hope they don't come pillaging to my house, but I would chase them away and get their loincloths and clubs with nails in my Sealy teeth, and goodbye, trogs. Of course could belong to secret service. Oh, my mind boggles (Ma said I have a natural boggly mind). Had good old sniff through the nettles, but couldn't get a clue. Saw a moose; huge. It was on the path, but it charged away before we could get close. Good job too, or I would have to rescue Ma again. That blessed vicious cat attack was enough the other day. Lots of 🐰🐇 fur everywhere; foxes' midnight snack. There it is most mornings; poor old rabbits 😦. Ma has asked me to amend two points. Jungle is woodland; moose is muntjac deer. She is very pedantic 🙄; she has never heard of writer's license 😦.

10th May 2022

Watergate. Well, here I am, all curled up, coat full of curls, still very damp. We were tramping about for well over an hour. Ma's idea: once out, just carry on. There's that Miss Ziggy Stardust—swear I heard her laughing. (She always looks miserable, but can't help her coat hanger mouth; just the way tortoises look. No amount of Botox can fix that you'd break the needle 😬.) She was happily basking under sunlamp, contemplating what to have for breakfast while we were contemplating on how wet we could get. Ma's waterproof coat turned out to be a washout 💦; see what I did there? Lawks alive, bury me bone, I am soooo funny 😦. Missed my calling; should have been a stand-up comic. Anyway, I hope you all have better weather than us 😦.

11th May 2022

Fledgling-gate. 🙄 Well, Ma was inside and heard me doing my urgent barking nonstop. Out she came to investigate. I had my illustrious nose jammed between two plant pots, giving forth. Nope, Ma couldn't see anything until she moved a pot and zoom, quick as a flash I was there. Flutter of feathers and a *sqwark*, Ma shouting "Cheese, cheese!" at the top of her voice, waving this block of cheese in front of me. (I will trade anything for a bit of cheese, usually). Well, that didn't work, so she grabbed the hose and turned it on. Immediately I flew back in. Of course I'm not frightened of the hose, but I'd just done my hair in a rather becoming quiff.

Ma's friend was about to visit, so back garden door was closed. First thing Ma asked her friend: "Can you touch birds?" To which her friend said yes. "Great," Ma said dragging the poor woman through the front door. Outside we went. I had to show where it had relocated (I was loving this, the hunter in me all alert). Bird found. Friend picked it up. Whoosh—yup, without my super-Sealy cloak, I snatched it so quickly they wondered where it had gone 😦. In my mouth of course. They started shouting. Lawks alive, bury me bone. I spat it out 😖. Well, it was moving in my mouth 😳😳😳. First time I had had a live thing in my mouth. So Ma went for the hose pipe again, and her friend picked it up. It was a young fledgling, worn out, terrified, so it was returned safely to the honeysuckle hedge. Panic over; what a performance. You see Ma has a thing about feathers and bones and cannot touch them. So, looking forward to a panic-stricken summer with fine sport for me. I only want to play with them 😇.

16th May 2022

Spagate. Well, off to hairdresser's. Susie picked me up. I pleaded and pleaded for dreadlocks; heart set on them after I saw pic of those Hungarian herding dogs, thinking that would get me out of grooming. No; hair not long enough ☹. OK, how about a blue or purple hair dye? Lots of humans have those. *No*, of course. I was so disappointed; I could have been the first purple Sealy. A guy can dream. Ma was happy—happy Ma, happy Sealy 🐶.

Then vet's this afternoon. Love going there; free six-month check-up, cos Ma's got me in their vet plan. Full bill of health. Vet pleased I had a waist 😳. It's not much of one. Glad it was duly admired, though.

Busy day flat out after this. Must say finding typing much easier now I've had my paws trimmed and manicured. Hope you all have had a good Monday. Bye from the Brockster 🐶.

17th May 2022

Magic treegate. Just look what I found all by myself. It's a semidetached tree house dwelling. Do you see the little doors? No numbers, so don't know how they (whoever, whatever they are) get any post. Probably got special coding. They have a lovely front garden. I thought I would help the flowers along. Well, they looked very dry, so performed *my* magical watering ceremony (don't forget my real name: Magical Duke) 😇. Wouldn't Ma sound silly calling that name out 🐶😅? Then, lawks alive, bury me bone 😳, saw one of my horse friends with a lady sitting on top of it in the paddock. My horse language very limited, but I tried to ask, "Are you all right? Just throw her if she's too heavy." Didn't work. I watched in helpless horror. I looked at Ma, and she said that it was fine and that she did a lot of it when she was younger. Yes, she assured me, they had been invented then.

Well-ll, ahhh. I have a cunning plan. The circus comes to town in the summer. You all know how I want to be in the circus; had my case packed last year, ready to run away with them 🐶 until Ma clocked it. Now if I can get Miss Ziggy Stardust to ride on my back as the first glamorous tortoise bareback rider (she can have a tutu and a bow on her head), I will have to bear the pain of the claws digging into my skin. We might even get on the TV. Well, a Sealy can dream. Don't think Ma would let us be a double act, cos no matter how you dress her up, she still looks like a porkpie with legs. Tough-looking legs at that. And I am not to be trusted with anything resembling food 😖, whether it's got a pulse or not (and an empty tortoise shell on my back wouldn't have the same impact). So I will pretend I don't know what's in the large box on the table 😅as Ma talks into it and puts food into it, while I sit on the top of the settee right nearby, pretending not to notice. She's not aware of our conversations, although the Stardust's knowledge not as extensive as mine 😖🐶. But I am trying to educate her 🐶. Phew, my paws are aching. Ma said far too long; people will give up halfway through. 🐶 Hope not.

18th May 2022

Lord of Misrule-gate. Well, it all started so well. Met a young whippersnapper beagle, just a wee pup (literally that's what he did when I said hello to him, uncalled for, but only young; probably overawed by meeting a super-Sealy). His ma was telling mine what a naughty pup he was. Ma, reassuring, told her I was a shocker, but how good I am now. *Mistake*: plans were forming in my mind. I'll play a joke on her today 😂🤡. So I just lay down on the grass, waiting for passers-by; nobody. So had a roll, kicking my legs, staring at her, laughing tongue right out (that was me, not Ma).

Then a postie appears—not the girls, but I have taught him I need treats, so yum: success. Later, Ma's friend visited, told not to leave her bag on the floor. Too late; off I ran with her mask like a flash. Mask retrieved, duly back in the bag; bag firmly zipped up, back on the floor 😆. Ma did warn her friend that I can unzip things. Well, joy. I ran, shoving her bag in front of me with my big black schnozzle before they could reach me. Unzipped, mask out, me off up the stairs, being chased with Ma shouting, "Cheese!"—waving a slab of extra mature cheddar in her hands. Cornered me in our bedroom, negotiations took place, and exchange made.

This afternoon Ma had to defrost little freezer, so out everything came. Two roast potatoes fell out of a bag. Don't ask me how I did it, but I got both of them in my mouth at once. Mmmmm— no, not giving these up so easily. Race around garden and house, oblivious to cheese offers. I got cornered in our bedroom and literally mouth prised open. I can usually win, but my mouth was so full, I had to surrender my prize.

Back down now; what to do next. Washing brush fell on the floor. Off I went again. Course, I let Ma have that when she caught me; tasted horrible anyway. When I saw the empty freezer, my heart fell through the floor. Lawks alive, bury me bone, no food. So I let Ma know just how I felt about that. Final straw. Not my fault, but expect I'll get the blame. Ma nearly strangled herself trying to get the rotary washing line thingy up. After three attempts she gave up; that's put her in a grump. So diplomatically I lay by her feet and went to sleep. Must get my energy levels up for tonight whilst she's watching tele for more fun and games 🤣😂😺😸.

20th May 2022

Hatgate. Look what I found—a pink hard hat. Really good find. I carried it around for a while, but when Ma said I couldn't start a hat collection, I spat it out. Ummmph. Yesterday another prize find: a little sun hat with lots of mice pics on it. Ma said it was a Mickey Mouse hat; it was small but would swamp a mouse 😳. Didn't know mice wore sun hats; must just be this Mickey that does. Met up with the "pug boys". Actually they have proper names—Boris and Dylan—but pug boys sounds like a couple of tough guys, and I can pretend we are in a gang. They have a tough look about them, and I have a swagger of a mobster; just my flight of fancy of course. We had a sniffing session and then went our separate ways. Back home hatless 😕😸.

21st May 2022

What a lovely Saturday. Lovely long walk; took ages just to get down the main road. Lots of fuss from people, even a treat from a nice man. Then it was a stand-up game/dance with a lovely female Airedale that was a stretch; she was all legs. Then a bit of excitement for me: I tracked down a mystery creature and started digging. Really enjoyed that until spoilsport Ma stepped in. My head was just on the way down to have a real good roll, but she said I mustn't go any further, as there was probably a poor creature quivering in fear, listening to a super-Sealy trying to get to it. Dragged away literally, as no way did I want to give up my first hunt 😔. Down the track in the woods saw a muntjac deer. Ma's lead arm was suddenly stretched (her knuckles nearly drag on the ground now, her lead arm is so stretched). Off I went, but it disappeared into the undergrowth. Hmm, not much fun.

On the way home for dinner this afternoon, going past the horses' paddocks, mmmmm: there on the ground was horse pooh, lots of it. Whoosh—quick as you like, I grabbed a mouthful. Yummy. I got carted off, still munching away. Gorgeous hors d'oeuvre (see what I did there? 😋😂) before kibble and beef. Further along the path met a playful young Lab. Ma warned Lab's ma about what lay on the path, but too late. My new friend had filled herself already. We had good sniff around each other, but for once we concentrated on the mouth area, our breaths fragrant.

Gardening after dinner. Of course I helped; bit of a failure this time, as the plant pot I ran off with was clean. Better luck tomorrow. Enjoy your Saturday evening; hope I let Ma enjoy hers 😂🙃😋.

25th May 2022

Fairgate. I got sooo excited when I saw what had sprung up overnight. Thought it was the 🎪 circus, but no—a funfair. I begged Ma to take me down for some rides on the roundabouts when it was ready and open. She told me that not even super-Sealies were allowed on the rides. I really fancied those little cars that bump into each other. I as you know, am a fully qualified co driver when we go in the car. So with blocks on those pushy things on the floor so I can reach them, I would be fine. Even offered to forgo my pocket money to pay the man at the fair (I do quite well at scrounging treats of people we meet anyway). "*No*; now enough," I was told, so I lay down on the grass and refused to move 😂. When Ma tried to get me upright, I put my tongue out, laughing and waving my legs in the air, rolled onto my back. This I might say is quite a familiar sight if I don't like the way we are going, etc. It always ends with a very fancy exaggerated commando crawl. Passers-by think it's so much fun 😋. Ma gives a weak grin 😅. Note pair of shorts again; made to leave them there on the bush. I could start up a charity shop, all the clothes I find: BROCK'S CHARITY, I could call it. Entrepawneer always thinking of new ideas. Well, going to work on Ma now. Will try whining and whinging, see if she changes her mind 😋♡   .

25th May 2022, continued …

Explosiongate 😱. Well, Ma and I were in bed, and suddenly she started exploding big time—about five times on the run. Lawks alive, and bury me bone, I was shocked to my core. I really get upset thinking she's going to explode. She was in disintegrating mode, so kept up whining and making a fuss of her. I did CPR training as soon as she picked me up as a baby. Took one look at her and thought, *I am going to be a care dog when I grow up*, but we love each other very much and understand each other. I must admit I am a very complex super-Sealy, but Ma has got to know everything I ask of her, no matter what. Poor women is like a yoyo, up and down after me, but I know she understands Sealy ways.

Just one thing puzzles me. Why are we a rare breed? That awful bossy man master trainer who came when I was young said on first sight as I was going berserk greeting him—I was a baby puplet, for goodness' sake—and he looked at Ma and said, "You wonder why they are a rare breed" 😱 Ma's face was a picture; thought she was going to lambaste him one 😋😆🤣. But before he left, he did say I was a lovely boy and very intelligent, as I picked things up quickly (that applies to anything that drops to the floor as well), 🤪 "so that made him worth all that money." Anyway I seem to have settled to sleep without any more explosions. She calls it hay fever. That's that Uppity Miss Ziggy Stardust's fault; her bedroom is hay with edible flowers, if you please 🤡. Hopefully off to sleep dream about the funfair. Now nearly midnight. All Ma's fault. Nighty-night, peeps 🤡.

28th May 2022

Cowgate. Yesterday lovely country walk. Saw another muntjac deer. Lots of my pals too. And coming back we interrupted a cow council in the next field; very important (I speak a little cow-speak) serious discussions about going on a milk strike unless they get extra treats, as fed up with eating grass. The head cow told us in no uncertain terms, "No pics, keep moving", so off we went.

In the afternoon we went to Auntie Pat's. Mollie, her spaniel, didn't want to play, so after running around the garden, I wandered inside and jumped up on the settee 😳♡ ♡ ♡ 🤡. What a shock. I was gazing at the most beautiful handsome super-Sealy. wow if I only looked like that. He didn't speak, just stared. Didn't know Auntie Pat had a secret Sealy. Can't wait for next visit to see if he's still there.

This morning it was cattle market day; *more* cows. Course Ma in her element (not forgetting her claim of growing up with cows 😅). They were making such a row. I just wanted to get in there. Maybe Ma would buy me one for an early birthday present; it would be my best friend. Plenty of room on our bed, as Ma only clings to the edge of our king-size bed. I would call her Daisy, and we could take her to the cow council. You guessed it: *no* 😔. So short-lived dreams like so many of my entrepawneer ideas. One day🤡🤡🤡. Happy Saturday, all.

31st May 2022

I had lovely walk this morning. Met lots of pals old and new, and I have rather taken to little people in pushchairs. I make them laugh; occasionally try to pinch a sock from a dangling foot. Ma always asks permission from their ma's first if I can say hello. On the way home this morning saw a lady with her doodly dog sitting by the war memorial, so thought good idea. Said howdy-doody to the doodle and lay down beside her on the grass. Left Ma standing like a spare part holding my lead. Busy; interesting. Lots of people passing by. I got a lot of attention, even a treat 😋😋😋.

Smiling people, so of course had to treat them to my routine, whether they liked it or not commando crawling, rolling over, kicking my legs gaily in the air, laughing with my tongue hanging out. Grand finale: more commando crawling. A bit limited, I know, sooo I'm going to take up juggling as well. That will be a challenge. Thought of doing it while on a unicycle, but second thoughts. Didn't like the idea of my ample Sealy bot on that thin saddle. Don't think my insurance covers dastardly life-changing accidents due to unicycle saddles. All of this, of course, will be useful for my circus act audition when they come this year, seeing as how I was banned from the funfair last year.

Helping Ma in the garden just know—lawks alive, and bury me bone—bee attack. Just like that, I had to come in, as I was leaping about snapping at them. Last year we had to have pest control in, as they nested under the shed floor. I get paranoid when a van comes with PEST CONTROL on the side, hoping the neighbours don't think it's for me. As if 🙃😵🐶. Happy Weds to all.

5ᵗʰ June 2022

Trumpetgate. If I never hear another trumpet again, I will be a happy Sealy 🙀🙀🐶. Fast asleep by Ma's feet, and lawks alive, and bury me bone, I nearly put a hole in the ceiling. The trumpet fanfare nearly gave me a heart attack😳, I kid you not. Whoever invented that dreadful instrument? There they were: fancy-dressed men all in a row, blowing like mad at some big church. Well, I have sort of got used to it as Ma's been glued to the TV, watching the jubilee all weekend, but *not a trumpet fan*. I am a very sensitive soul.

Ma likes creepy violent thriller things on TV, and the music is very scary, so I munch my bones even louder. Maybe I could suggest earmuffs for my birthday, but don't want to appear a scaredy-cat. Dreadful expression 😖🐶.

8ᵗʰ June 2022

Thursdaygate. Well, first I found this alien object. I think it's a micro spaceship, so look out for mini aliens. I wasn't allowed too near it; contamination possible 😳. Farther down the road, *vulture attack*. I had to protect Ma, as somebody was throwing chicken bits in the road for them—dead chicken, obvs. Flocks of gulls following the vulture—uh-uh; OK, Ma: kites. Hmmmph; not so exciting, but OK. It swooped down to the road to get the chicken before I had a chance. Then we saw a duck creche. Couldn't get too close; Ma ducks, lots of babies. Their dads were watching from the lake.

Met a new mate a whipoodle. Yup, guys, you heard it here first. Getting quite a complex. Asked Ma if I could pretend to be a Sealyoodle. "*No, my boy. Be proud of your heritage.*" Subject closed. I am proud; just wanted to pretend to fit in with the majority of the local guys 😔.

Ma got savaged by the shell disaster Miss Ziggy Stardust yesterday. Mistook end of her finger for carrot. Nasty 🐷🐯, short-sighted, although I hear she's arranging for blue contact lenses. 😩😩😩 Sight for sore eyes 😂. See what I did there? She thinks she will look more glamorous 😂🤡. Having words later with her. Ma wouldn't wear a sling, as she said it's fine. I thought it would be more dramatic, a sling, but there you go. Happy Thursday 🤡.

10th June 2022

Beardgate. Well, what a morning. Something was in the air; I could sense it 🤨. I decided to lengthen the walk by laying down on the grass, kicking my legs in the air, and commando crawling. Often then I posed for a pic on the park bench, then through the woods back. Every peemail was full of classified information; still do a little undercover agent work for Big Chief Sealy 🕵️🕵️ on the side, so really took time to take it on board.

Then I met a very cute little girl, Daisy. She was a chijack 😊. Yup, not a poodle or a doodle in sight 🤣. She was petite but lovely Chihuahua/Jack Russell, smaller than my head. Played around, then back home. Strange—after my drink of water, didn't get undressed. Still trussed up in my male bra, as I call my harness and collar, and huddled into downstairs loo. *Then* I spotted it, as the door was firmly shut behind us: bowl of water on the floor 🙀. Knew it was a bad day to get up. Sponge, shampoo, and towel all laid out on the floor. Struggle? Oh you betcha. Not taking this lying down. Lawks alive, and bury me bone, Ma was *forcing* me to have a beard shampoo. No matter how I wriggled, the look of grim determination on her face was horrific to see. *Assault*, I call it. at last my traumatic ordeal came to an end. How can I hold my head up now? My beard was of interest to all my mates. They loved to have second-hand sniffs of the collection of smells I have carefully garnered. Now to dirty it up as soon as possible. I think this was payback as Ma has taken up art 🙈, as she calls it, after she hasn't done any since she got me, and she had started a pic of me. White paint and ink, and on the way to my lookout post on the back of the settee, I put my big fat paws, as she said—rude, I thought—right in the middle of wet painting 🤡, adding a personal touch, as I told her. But from the look on her face, well, mmmm, she wasn't a happy bunny. Happy Friday, you all 🤡🤣🙈🤡.

13th June 2022

Thrapston Lakes. Lovely walk; beautiful place. Found a fox hole or badger sett, as quite big. Ma refused to let me have a look-see further than the edge Then, joy of joys, met my mate Rufus, the spaniel purebred; not a doodle in sight. He's such fun. Ma let me off the lead so I could race around with him. I did, and please note: kept up with him. His pa was amazed at my turn of speed. Put my turbojets on 😂. After a while we made our way home *off the lead* through the woods. When I was a young lad, I did wander off, so been confined ever since to lead walks. But hopefully I have proved I can be a good boy—well, sometimes. It's 2.7 miles around the lake and lots of smells. Still can't find that fox pooh, though; will keep looking. Happy Monday 🤡.

14th June 2022

Lakegate. Early morning going around the lake look at me off lead 🙄. Couldn't resist looking back at Ma; that was short-lived. Soon running like a loony, exploring side tracks. Ma heard a large splash 😵 and came racing—well, walking quickly😅—only to find me on the bank, and guess what I had roused: a large evil swan 🦢 into the water. I came running back to Ma laughing at my joke 🐶😆. Well, met some great guys and had races and games. We were a pack of four for some way—three spaniels and me, soon joined by a 😊 doodle girl. She was rather taken with my swagger, I think; big black schnozzle and flicked-back ears helped. We ran races. Great walk, as in the shade most of the time.

The indignity of it all. When we got home, I was taken straight out into the garden and hosed— yes, *hosed*. My feet and legs had got very dirty. Well, I put up a song and dance, as you can imagine, worthy of a super-Sealy. It was worth it, and off the lead. I did disappear couple of times, but came back😁😁😁. Only drawback is getting up early ☹. We had a vanguard of butterflies and dragonflies/copter 🚁 flies—bright blue—again following us along. We had a lovely walk; tuna and kibble waiting for me at home after the hosedown 😍☹🐶.

16th June 2022

Lakegate again. Sooo hot last night, had to come down and sleep on the settee, even though Ma had two fans directed at me; no expense spared 😍. It will all cool down, as I am expecting a new cool mat from a place called Amazon.

Most of my walk I had a doodle chap with me, running around playing tic and exploring down by the lakeside, which made Ma quite twitchy. She's scared of water. Can't swim, you see. Reckons if I fell in and got into trouble, she'd be useless. No change there; just got a telling off for being rude 😵😵😵. Ma looking over my shoulder. I briefly disappeared for a short while 😍. That put the wind up her. Well, it was the sighting of a hairy rat begging to be chased. Of course it ended safely up a tree. So well-behaved, didn't even snack on the horse 🐴 poop that was on the path. Looked tempting; shouldn't have been there, as horses not allowed. Aha—maybe it was a huge alien monster that only comes out at night for the huge mounds on the path. It must feel better—better out than in. I say 😊. Got recognised for what I am today by a clever lady 🐶🐶. Resting up now. Happy hot Friday 🐶♡.

24th June 2022

Pushchairgate. Well, just lookee. See what we came across on our walk 🙄: alert dog abandoned in a pushchair. I know him—it was Ted (one of Ma's groomer's dogs), and I do have pushchair envy. But Ma said, "Just be glad you can use your legs." Of course we rushed to the rescue, and of course his dad was jawing away to someone in a car, so he was safe. It was the look on his face ☹. So I went and licked him, did a commando crawl, hoping to cheer him up. Think it worked. Shame my juggling clubs were at home. That really would have worked. Must admit I do drop the odd one🐶. Nearly killed a miniature Yorkie once 😵☹.

Ma left me in charge and went out to Thrapston Charter Fair this afternoon. I did ask, but she said *no*. It was hot and busy, and all I would see was a sea of legs; no fun for me. So had a one-sided conversation with scaly-faced Miss Ziggy Stardust, who had actually gone to bed. So really had to shout, as she buries herself under her hay. Really bored, and Ma had taken her phone, so couldn't even post anything. And no passers-by, as they had all passed by going to the Charter Fair, so nobody to hurl insults or greetings at, depending on who they were. Have a happy weekend to one and all 😃.

26th June 2022

Hi, guys. Been to paddock playschool; great stuff. Had a man here this morning to look at our fridge, which knocked all the electrics out in the kitchen last night. Lawks alive, and bury me bone, my food is in there. Panic stations. Anyway, all working now, but fridge sticking out not where it usually is. Ma not thrilled, but see how we go.

Yesterday I saw a strange sight: a very tall man, think he might have been a giant, with the tiniest of pups, one on either side of him. Twelve-week-old miniature sausage dogs, although so tiny, more of a chipolata if you ask me. I just stared. Rude, I know. I stood really still in case I trod on them, and let them fuss around me. Must admit they were very sweet. Two policemen were also spotted. Now this was a rare sighting of the elusive long arm of the law; more elusive than that fox poo I am in search of. I would love to have a playmate, but no. Ma said sorry, but I am going to be an only pup 🐼.

29ᵗʰ June 2022

Well, we went a lovely two-village walk today. Out for ages. Saw a corpse: half a crow. Was I allowed to investigate it? Certainly not. Stopped my collection of corpses for my nature table—really, my best hobby; gone down the chute. Ma under the weather. Did a test thing this morning for Covid, but it was negative. I told her probably fluey cold again and hay fever. Studied a bit of medicine, so know what I'm talking about .... a bit 😁.

Anyway, we had to change the bed today. Of course I did my best to help. Ummmph 😵, lawks alive, and bury me bone, what can a guy do, right? I was sitting in the middle of the clean sheet, which didn't go down well. Persuaded Ma to have a lay-down, and I put on a cabaret for her. Tossed my bone in the air so it narrowly missed her head. Did bed surfing commando crawling, making lovely howly sounds. Finale was a mammoth Sealy sit, which I held for ages. You guessed it; cheered Ma up. Bed still not made, but as I said to Ma, it ain't going anywhere; we can do it later. Just done formula-one dash around house and garden and ready for afternoon walk. Hope all your ma's are well. It falls to us to be their carers when needed. Did suggest her going to doc's, but she said it would be quicker and easier to see my doc 😂🤣🐼.

7ᵗʰ July 2022

Come on, Ma—seven a.m. I can't wait to beat the heat and get down to the woods and lake. Heard that pesky noise again, but not worried now. I know it's the deers. Must say they do leave funny smells around; makes me cough sometimes.

Walking along when cyclist appeared. Never met one when I have been off lead before. I ran alongside for a bit, then got fed up and came back to Ma. *No ankles* were harmed. Met a grumpy Labrador, who told me to wipe that silly grin off my face and show her the respect she deserved, so gave her a wide berth, flicking my ears inside out over my shoulders, and swaggered past, tongue out Saturday to you, Ms Grumpy.

Ma not a happy bunny positive for Covid this morning after negative yesterday, and can't go to the barbie at the top of the road this evening. So I'm going to have to pull some tricks out of the hat to cheer her up. Miss Ziggy Stardust has done a few backflips 🐢; got stuck at one point, flippers rotating. she nearly took off and sang Ma a tortoise song, which of course was silent 😵, but we are doing our best. Happy Saturday, folks 😝🐼.

13ᵗʰ July 2022

Fed up, neglected, ignored. You do all you can for your ma's, nurse them through darn Covid when nobody wants to come within an arm's length apart from Dr Brock (yes, I can use my title when in medical mode). Dance hand and paw looking after her, sharing my kibble, offering my chews, above and beyond expectations. *Then* feeling better, out in the garden she goes, throwing burnt plants out, muttering to herself. Fine, but it's the dead snaky thing that suddenly bursts into life, spurting water; hmmmp. "Indoors, my lad; you had to suffer that this morning on my carefully nurtured filthy legs" 😳. Now of course she's too tired for anything. Hopefully can summon up the strength to give me my dinner 🤤. Oh, and of course evening treats. I have my ways to remind her if she does forget, you betcha. Happy Wednesday ♡🐶.

13th July 2022, continued ...

Sandal scandal 😳. Well, today started well 😎. Restless in the night, so on and off our bed to start with. Ma found her sandal in the hall this morning—*chewed.* 🙀🙀🙀 Who could have done that? I got it waved in my face. Well, I took a dutiful sniff, looked, and trotted off, ears flicked back, tail held high, picture of innocence 😇. Ma asked me outright, "Who did this?" 😤 Well, Miss Ziggy Stardust 🐹could have climbed out of her run, couldn't she ? 🤗 No! That didn't wash 😌. Well, quite frankly, I was driven mad by the heatwave and didn't know what I was doing. All a blur, really, and so my day began. Lakeside walk; lots of pals met up with and races and paddling in the lake, sending killer super-Sealy frowns at the evil king swans gliding on the lake. Beautiful heron took off, and we were escorted by a platoon of chopperflies (may flies remind me of 🚁), bright blue dazzling colour (think Ma's forgotten about the sandal). Thoroughly hosed down; still put up a struggle. Well, you have to, don't you? Happy Thursday; keep cool ♡   🐶.

14th July 2022

Feathergate. Well lawks alive, and bury me bone, what the .... Evil swan's feather on the path. Is it a trap? Is the owner peering at me through the rushes, ready to come rushing and hissing at me—swan attack? Cripes, it stinks. Had to put Ma back on the lead as a precaution. Besides, I wasn't moving😳; had to be dragged away. Oh, there is danger lurking behind every clump of reeds and rushes; rest assured.

Met lots of mates. Had a bit of fun: joggers, cyclists (none were injured as they passed by). This was just gone 6.30 a.m.; busy, busy—all of us trying to escape the heat. "Mad dogs and Englishmen go out in the midday sun," as the saying goes, and as you all know I'm far from mad 😤😝. Foxes were busy last night. There was rabbit fur scattered around; few bunny Maltesers around to snack on (prebreakfast). Stay cool ♡   🐶.

16th July 2022

Up at the crack; again, heat beating. Barking deers loud this morning—what a racket. Through the woods to the lake saw this amazing tree. After watering it, asked Ma about it. She said magical meeting tree for fairies, elves, and little creatures to meet in the dark and discuss preservation of their woods and ways to stay hidden from human eyes and nosy Sealies. Pshhhht; don't believe her. Think the heat's got to her 😎. Lawks alive, and bury me bone, what the devil was that? A thing with long ears and fluff bob of a tail hopping around 😳🐰🐿. Looks worth chasing, whatever it is, but quickly put Ma back on the lead. Can't have her running after unknown alien creatures. Well, Ma explained it was a rabbit really 😯, and apparently they are Malteser factories on legs. Hmmmph; fancy that. Must say, enjoy the odd snack on the way around the lake. It was my first sighting of a rabbit. Met two basset hound boys; crikey. Hefty guys, really heavy, on short stumpy legs. Not seen them before. Happy smiley chaps though. Had great games with a young Staffy girl. Eventually got to my watering hole and had a paddle-waddle and back for brekkie; tuna and kibble. Have a lovely Saturday, one and all; stay cool 😎. Yes, I actually had to wear my shades this morning ♡ 🐶.

18th July 2022

Black legs 🐾🐾🐾🐾. Got really filthified at the lakes this morning. Very pleased with myself; look quite the action Sealy (course I know the consequences; hosepipe, see you soon 😵). I adopted a lady walker this morning. Felt so sorry for her. She was dogless 😟. So trotted briskly alongside her. Kept looking up to see if it was making her happy. In the end Ma had to attach herself to me, and we waited by the lake a while till she'd gone. Off again; met my two Pointer sisters, and whayee, off we went, into the lake and dashing about. Hmmm. second time Ma had to collect me 😵. Just couldn't help myself. Actually, my hosepipe experience was quite enjoyable. Had to squeak and make weird noises as though I was being tortured—well, you have to, don't you? So fluffy white Sealy again. Ma's friend Frances bought some veg up from their allotment, so I made a big fuss of her. Loved her; gave a Sealy sit-up and sloppy kisses. Now back to fangate and cold mat. Keep cool and safe, everyone ♡ ❄ .

18th July 2022, continued …

Well, what a night 😱. Ma wandering around at all hours, Sat in the garden at one a.m.; fans going—phew. Up very early this morning around the lakes. I was a good boy; met some lovely pals, also the two sheepdogs from next door, and one of them is called Badger, so in our close we have Brock and Badger 🦡😂. Well, made me laugh. Filthified really well; getting quite the expert, *and* I think I'm looking forward to the hosing down bit at home in this weather. Miss Ziggy Stardust got her own heat from her lamps, gorging on tomato 🍅, strawberry 🍓, and watermelon 🍉. Yuck. Had to leave a corpse on my walk this morning; feathers everywhere and a portion of ??—whatever. It had been laying right under my schnozzle, *but* was allowed to carry a dead leather flip-flop around, so not a fruitless morning after all. Stay cool, my friends ♡ 🐶.

20th July 2022

Well, what a lovely walk, all the way around the lake, with a new friend from the next town: a very handsome Gordon setter nine months old. So I was the senior here. Ummmph. He was so well trained 😎. Ah well. We ran mad races, chased each other, and lots of water bombing in the lake (must have made the evil swan things look twice). Of course he was a lot taller than me; not a problem 😆. His pa and grandma were very interesting people, so Ma was happy too. They are as vocal as us—they never stopped 😄. Very busy. Saw lots of mates, but of course couldn't stop long to chat, just a polite expected bum sniff and off again.

Not drinking enough for Ma's liking, so she's boiling my chicken breasts in a lot of liquid and pouring it over my kibble, so fluid intake up. Happy Wednesday; bring on the cooler weather.

Can't imagine how my Newfie friend Tilly is with all that thick hair. Off for a snooze now ♡ ♡ 🐼.

Oh—P.S. Happy birthday, Miss Ziggy Stardust. Hope you liked the birthday card of me I sent you 😹😹 (bet she didn't). I thought it a very personal touch 😇.

21ˢᵗ July 2022

Back on the cool mat. "Up and at 'em," Six thirty a.m. walk in the *rain*, yup, rain. Road walk again, but needed to catch up on peemails on my old pre-heatwave route. Panic in the kitchen on our return: my chicken had gone off ☹. Fridge playing up again, so Ma is going to bite the bullet and get a new one for me. Later Ma went out hunter-gathering, foraging for food. Honestly, she's going to Aldi. You'd think she was going out with a rifle into darkest Africa—😂. Delusions of grandeur, don't you think 😹? She also went fridge hunting with all the measurements except the width 😂. *Typical*. Got to be right, as fits into alcove. I was left holding the fort with Miss Ziggy Stardust; she was being very stroppy and rude to me. She's all smiles and sweetness in front of Ma; two-faced scalyface 😒. Anyway, the posh moisturizer that Ma gave her for her birthday is not working. She thinks it is and told me she was going to ask Ma for a mirror in her bedroom. Cruel to be kind; I told her, "Don't bother"; cracked glass in her hay bedding not a good idea. Well, back to snoozing until afternoon walk, as pavement not hot, and home for dinner with food that's not gone off. Happy Friday, folks ♡ 🐼.

23ʳᵈ July 2022

Long walk this morning. Ma slept in until six thirty, but it was cool. Met some pals and a Staffie that gave me a mouthful of the worst swear words I have ever heard, and do you know, I just looked away in disdain (anybody swears around here, it's me!). I tossed my head, stood on tippytoes, and swaggered past, flicking my left ear inside out (it's quite the fashion, don't you know). Next along was a great big American bully with cropped ears, so obviously an immigrant. She too glared at me, but they had crossed over the road. Hope my super-Sealy killer frown reached her—just a warning. Down by the river the ground was littered with evil swan kings' feathers 🤕. Next along came a cockapoo. Ma was asked what I was crossed with by the owner 🙄, so he got the tale of the Sealyhams whether he wanted it or not. Saw a heron, and the ducks came to see us. Thought we had bread for them. So after posting this, going to crash out. Happy Saturday.

24ᵗʰ July 2022

Nope, not coming down. Physically assaulted to get this cool coat on, cornered and wrestled to the ground, captured in my bedroom. Lawks alive, and bury me bone, what the heck. Auntie Pat been here for visit. Ma gave her some of her medicine, which seemed to cheer both of them up. Must be "happy juice", and I chewed my bone sitting on top of Auntie Pat. It was great fun; every time I dropped it, I gave pitiful whine, and hey presto, it was handed back to me. Ma said I had only child syndrome 🙃. Think she meant spoilt. *Rude*, don't you think? I gave them both a really good face wash, so they should be grateful for that. Well, if Ma can tempt me back downstairs, I will have my dinner. At the moment typing this post in the safety of our bedroom, though doesn't matter, as assault over; deed done. Cold coat on. Ma should have been a rugby player 😕♡ 🐶.

27th July 2022

Met human and doggy friends this morning, and weather much kinder. All around our town on the paths there are dog bowls and kitchen bowls full of water for us. Ma always carries a bottle of water and collapsible drinking bowl when I take her out for her walk, but I only have sips. But if I see the communal ones standing there, I slurp happily away and come up with a soaking wet beard. I just like alfresco drinking; besides, only polite, as people are being kind. Sorry, guys, if I leave the water a bit scummy after a beard wash, but us bearded boys can't help it. I am now in control of my cat issues (most of the time), and after giving my best super-Sealy killer frown, trot in, tail curled right over my back. Glad we get to keep our tails. Ma said in the old days we had them taken off. Must say I do chase it a bit sometimes, but Ma stops me, saying only mad dogs do that 🤪😁. Hope you all had a good Wednesday ♡   ♡   🐶.

29ᵗʰ July 2022

Early walk today, as Ma has to go to hospital for knee and thumbs injections, soooo I'm in sole charge of the house and of course Miss Ziggy Stardust (who would have it the other way round 😵). On our walk encountered Queen Swan and her swanlets, which entailed lots of hissing and warnings from nasty old Ma swan. I of course was on standby in attack mode, just in case of a swan charge 🦢. Ma's got to rest her leg; do only tiny round the block tonight, so I'm going to have her on a short lead. Finding teasels a huge nuisance at the moment; seem to leap at me and tangle up in my fur. Have to stop and get unravelled. Not a good look: matted knotted beard with a teasel in the middle of it. Salon day Monday; looking forward to it. New look: I want hair straightening and a purple rinse (???), dreadlocks in my beard, but think it's not long enough. Looking to up the street cred ✌️ 😎😵🤡.

30ᵗʰ July 2022

Well, what a lovely surprise. Ma's great granddaughter came to see me with her ma and pa and Ma's son. Haven't seen Fiadh since I was pushchair escort for her. Ohhh, love ♡ her. She just wanted to touch me. Even let her pull my beard a bit; got my own back, as ran off with her dummy 😵😂, but that was short-lived. I think I would make a great childminder; new string to my bow. Poor little Fiadh had a cold. Mini explosions not as loud as Ma, thank goodness.

What a day. New fridge delivered at the crack of dawn—well, 8.45 a.m., so been a busy day Ma and I have had a happy day. 🤩♡ 🤡 Miss Ziggy Stardust missed it all as went back to her bedroom quite early. She will be so cross I've got one over her 🤭🐑.

1ˢᵗ August 2022

The signs were all there! This morning 😖 half a watermelon fell out of fridge face down, splat on the kitchen floor. Air went blue 😤. The hand clippers Ma has for me fell off the shelf—busticated. Blue air again 😤. The third disaster to come later. Susie picked me up and my pampering began. If you really stare very hard at me, touch of the lurgy that Dalmatian thing infected me with is showing slightly, but must say my spots are Sealy spots, so superior. Then Ma said we were going to a car wash (thank god for that; only the muck and spiders cobwebs holding the car together—ashamed to be seen in it).

By now it was twelve thirty; sun had come out, so left car with the army of men waiting to wash them, and we went across to Barnwell Country Park. Not been before; normally wouldn't be out now 🌞, so kept to the shady bits. I met huge black Newfie called Zeus. Bit younger than me. Poor boy, thick long black hair. We had a friendly sniffy greeting. I of course not up to scratch with my newly pampered backside, but hey 😌, give it an hour or two.

Back to collect car. Ma waving her debit card about (third disaster coming up), but only take cash. *Of course they do* 😖. Back to nearest town money machine. Well, Ma was no way leaving me in the car. The men had offered to look after me; she wasn't having that, no way—nor was I 😨 —so nearest machine was Co-op shop. We stepped in, but it was at the back of the shop. Ma asked an assistant, "Could we just nip down to it?" *Can't have dogs in here.* Lawks alive, and bury me bone, I'm cleaner than you at the moment and I was already in there 😤. You can tie him up outside. *Rude,* really. Ma not having that either so trip around town to cash machine via the pet shop 😎. Bought me some treats and back to the car washers and home. *What a performance.* So fan full-on, the highest it can go, Ma clinging to the end of the settee looking as though she's in a tornado 🌪 . All's well that ends well. Hopefully quiet, uneventful evening ahead; paws crossed. Enough dramas for today 🤍 🤡🤍 .

6th August 2022

Drama Sunday. Well, it was all going well until it wasn't 😵‍💫🫣. Just after my roll around, I was up and tearing frantically at grass as much as I could. Lawks alive, and bury me bone, so something not right here. I was tearing and ripping the grass out, any sort of grass. Well, Ma got me in the car and 🤮 wallop all over the gear stick: bile and grass. Ma just got on with it, cleared it up, and home. I rushed straight through to the garden, ripping any weeds poking out of the slabs. Then ornamental grasses; went for a Burton pot and all. I was in "grass frenzy". Got hoiked back in; had a go at the carpet and anything lying on the floor.

Gulped whole bowl of water down and 🤮 back up. Ma phoned emergency vet up free appointment given then she thought about it. I was coughing and making odd Sealy noises; definitely mouth problem, nothing to see. She opened my mouth wide and had poke round. *Rude*, I thought 😤😤😤. All was OK until roll about, sooo ? Bitten by something in the grass—not snake, as all grass was parched. Allergic reaction, so Ma phoned vet again, as she wanted the say-so for antihistamine tab. Had one, then quietened down. Still ripping at grass if I went in garden, but settled. Went and had my dinner and another tab. Evening time did a lot of sleeping. Gulping a bit, but strained my throat vomiting probably. No treats in the evening, and didn't ask for any. One fifteen in the morning, leapt off our bed, and Ma took me out to have a wee around the block. She had made emergency appointment at my doc's (easier and faster than her doc's) this morning as soon as they were in, but cancelled when we were out walking. Things back to normal more or less, so cancelled my appointment. Spoke to vet: carry on tabs for couple of days. Frightened myself and Ma. Paddock playschool early tomorrow cos of weather; so happy not to miss that. Hope you all had a better Sunday than what we did 🤗. "Bad grammar, young Brock." Yup, Ma reading over my shoulder again; no privacy 🙄🤍 🤡. "Freedom of speech", Ma, ever heard of it? 😂🤣

8th August 2022

Bad boy 🤡. *Spotgate.* Just back from paddock playschool, early cos of heat. Not bad there, but 👀😐 oh my! Last night late walk, not only one spotted nemesis but two. Couldn't believe it. Where are all these Dalmatians coming from? It's a stitch-up. Strength draining to summon up such a tirade of insulting bad language and straining to get at them. I must admit I get tunnel vision, and a red mist descends; working on the foaming at the mouth with white spittle flying. That might frighten them. Must say they completely ignore me 😔 and trot.

Earlier Ma was walking down, chatting with friends, and we came upon a water bowl (it's always there; kind lady fills it every day) in the driveway. So stopped and took my fill as usual, and then 😵‍💫😵‍💫😵‍💫👀 don't know what came over me, but cocked my elegant leg and *bingo* peed straight into the water bowl, resulting in great splashes. Well, Ma and friends cracked up laughing;

couldn't help themselves, although naughty. Sooo that got more laughs than all my other tricks, so must keep 👀 peeled for more water bowls. Stay cool ♡ 😎😊.

11ᵗʰ August 2022

Morning, hauled off our bed at dawn 😵 and out, avoiding the heat of the day. Met some nice guys; risked a roll in the grass, hoping nothing lurking there to bite my mouth again. Dreadful night. Well, I slept; fan on head fan on bottom hair whipping around in the breeze (more like a hurricane, Ma said). She tethered herself down in the slipstream of the draught, but she was up again until two a.m. I was not moving; zzzzz. Done my post now, so neighbourhood watchdog duties on my cool mat with my own personal fan on full. Have a great day ♡ 🐶.

12ᵗʰ August 2022

Evil swan ma with her swanlets. I thought she looked miserable and bad-tempered, so did my rolling on my back, kicking my legs in the air act, grinning at her, tongue lolling out. *Wowee*, lawks alive, and bury me bone, she didn't appreciate that. No pics. As Ma was trying to drag me away, her wings rose above her head, and she hissed so loudly I could almost smell her swan breath 😖. Can't resist a bit of taunting though.😈😈

Further on, "He's a Sealyham, isn't he?" Sweet music to my flicked back ears (cooler that way, and more avant garde, methinks). Wow. Ma said apparently lady's a groomer but only seen Sealies at *crufts*, so got a lot of fuss there. Bit further on, "Is he Westie?" 😵😵😵😵 So Ma went into her spiel: *noooo*. Going under my own special fan now on my cool mat to dream of 🦆🦆🦆 fighting warrior swans (they are even worse and scarier than ordinary evil swans *and* ten times bigger and wear breastplates made of elvish metals 😕) ⚔️🐶. Oh, and of course I always win.

17ᵗʰ August 2022

This morning another early walk, as sun back out 😊. Came across a beautiful coloured abandoned 🏀 ball. Was I allowed a game? Oh no, belongs to some little child. Hmmmph. Shouldn't leave it lying about, I say. Later on I got told off as I stared really hard and refused to move, looking at a man with a very long straggly beard (shame on him; mine's very well groomed). He was sitting on the bench across the road with a can of drink (alcohol in his hand 8.30 a.m.). He looked like a Taliban person to me (saw a programme about them). Ma said she didn't think they drank alcohol so not to be silly. It worked though; out came a bit of biscuit to distract my super-Sealy stare (not my killer stare), so off I trotted, flicking an ear back over my neck. Mission accomplished. Although if he had come over to Ma, I was ready to bare my teeth and strive very hard to get a bit of foam spitting out of my mouth and give him a Sealy send-off, although must say not had to have done that yet. This is why I was so flaked-out tired at times, looking after Ma. Big responsibility, making sure she stays upright for starters. Never known any human to be so clumsy; she could trip over a feather. Anyway, back to my cooling mat and nap before dinner. Hope you all have a good Friday ♡ 🐶.

19ᵗʰ August 2022

Yumster. Stole chunk of ice from freezer, trying to make a statue of a Sealy out of it, but it melted too fast 😥. Well, gas boiler man came for routine boiler check. I gave him an uproarious greeting. He remembered me from last time 😗; really can't think why😵. His bag was very interesting; different tools. Wondered which one I could secret away. He was practically ignoring me, busy doing the boiler, so waste of time doing Sealy sit-ups or commando crawling, so decided to hump my bed 👀😱. (I don't make a habit of this by the way.) 😂 That worked. He was laughing as Ma was dragging me away from my bed, which I had a firm hold on, so we all went skidding across the kitchen floor. Ah well, "such is life. Life is such. If it wasn't for Brock, it wouldn't be much." 😂🐶♡   Happy Saturday, one and all. —Oh yes, Debbie our postie posted a letter for Ma, and guess what was on the mat. Yes, a bonio for me, so that letter was untouched by Sealy teeth ♡   🐶.

23ʳᵈ August 2022

Happy birthday to me 🎊🍄🦴. Raining c—ts and dogs, but, hey, look: two cards. Yes. Miss Ziggy Stardust (my tortoise) delivered, and a squeaky toy with pockets on it for treats. Eaten them 😸. Ma's got me beefsteak for dinner, and I had breakfast of kibbles with bits of cheese on it (it's all about the food as you fellow Sealies know).

Got woken up this morning by this wailing sound. Lawks alive, and bury me bone, what the 😱? Oh, stand down; just Ma singing Happy Birthday. I smiled, tongue lolling out trying to look thrilled at being woken up. Can't wait for rain to stop or ease, as my birthday badge from my card is on my harness😵, and want to show it off. Ma said I mustn't roll, as I don't want to stab myself. Happy Thursday, even though it's a wet one 🐶♡   .

61

26ᵗʰ August 2022

Hi. *Thank you, one and all,* for all my lovely birthday wishes. Couldn't believe it. I'm scarfing my steak (medium rare) and kibble. Ma enjoyed her pizza 😋 too. Believe that was well done (burnt). Asked Ma if I could wear my birthday badge, which is on my harness, for a few days. In fact, I'm calling it a medal; sounds better. Saw two ladies today who cuddled me and wished me happy birthday, for which they got a kiss with my big long tongue right in their mouths. (Ma didn't tell them where it had been before 😂😝.) Hope you all had a good Friday, and enjoy your weekend ♡   🐶.

29ᵗʰ August 2022

Such excitement. Little Fiadh and all my Labrador buddies came visiting. They went through all my toys, and black Monty had one of my chews. *C'est la vie*; I pinch their toys when I visit them. We all went for walk around the lake. Shame not going in, as algae still bad. We are both worn out now, but Ma and I so happy to see them all. At least I will give Ma quiet evening so she can watch picture box in peace. Happy bank hols ♡   🐶.

Yesterday was very, very exciting too. One of Ma's x colleagues, Gina, texted would we like to visit. So got picked up in a big car. Scary, really, as it made strange sounds if you got too near to obstacles. Magic car, I suspect. Our car just goes bump, no warning 😅. Well, new house to nose around, which I did vigorously, testing the bounciness of both settees 😵. Ma told me off, but had good nosy around before out into the garden. Beautiful; lots of things to water (heard there was a shortage, so helped out).

Then what did I spy but a handsome Sealy looking straight at me. Wow. Just like the guy in my own garden and in the oven door at home. Decided he is my guardian angel Sealy, always looking out for me. When I got home, rushed straight into my garden, and sure enough, he was there, staring right back at me with mutual admiration on his face. Ahhhh, so pleased he'd found his way back to my garden, and wasn't still at Ma's friend's garden I can rest easier now, knowing he hasn't deserted me. Happy Monday 🐶♡   .

29ᵗʰ August 2022, continued ...

Just got back from paddock playschool. Thank you, Dani and Emma. Dani took pics and sent them to Ma. I just need my super-Sealy cape, and I'm sure I could take off. Really enjoy myself there. Now then, last night Ma was watching a programme on the picture box, "House of Dragons." Got her to take a pic. You see, I always knew deep down that there really are dragons, and there's the proof. Sooo not only am I hunting yeti and aliens, now dragon hunting too; must keep eyes wide open 👀 when we go through the woods. Though not a good hidey place for dragons; woods wouldn't last long. Just a dragon hiccup or backfire (as I like to call my wind attacks) and no woods left 💨😱. Ma said I live in my own world of make-believe, and no wonder I get so excited (must admit I do get beside myself sometimes), but that's me ♡   .

Well, had a very busy weekend visiting being visited and reunited with my Labs (known and played with them since a tiny pup), ending up with playschool. Diary free until next Monday, now my pamper day with Susie. Try and get some dreadlocks going, as hair quite long now. Have a good week.

Afterthought—just said to Ma lack of molehills. Have they gone on summer hols? Have to have escorts and have white sticks or weeny guide ferrets to be with them. Food for thought 😜. Nap time now ♡ 🤡.

1ˢᵗ September 2022

Liberty of it. Minding my own business, contemplating what mischief to get up to, when Ma turfs me out in the garden, telling me to kill 🙄🫣 what? —Sparrows? I don't think so. Rats 🐀 spotted eating birdseed; all gone of course now. She said it was inbred in me and to do my job. Hello, lady, my day off. Think about it tomorrow 😌 .

4ᵗʰ September 2022

Post grooming. Just lookee: my colours are showing again, more on other side of my head too. I'm in navigation mode. Ma needs all the help she can get 😵. Got home had my bra, as I call my harness, taken off. Front door ajar. Whoosh, that's me out off through the door. Freeeedom! Ma told me she nearly had a fit. There was me naked, swaggering alone at a fast pace, ear flicked back, jack the lad. Anyway, by the time she had got my bra and a treat in her hand, she got to the door—hey, presto, who was this jaunty dog about town coming down the drive straight past her into the hall 🥴😂🥴? What a joke I played on her, although don't think she got it. Ah well, can't win them all. Hope you guys had a shower-free day. Brushed and combed within an inch of my life, even see my eyelashes under my eyebrows now ♡ 🐼.

10ᵗʰ September 2022

Horsegate. Well, Ma and I very concerned about the horse lying down in the next field, as we're its friends. Hopefully its owner will be here soon. They come every morning. In the second field was a zebra; couldn't believe my Sealy eyes 👀. Had it escaped from a zoo? And what had it done to my friend who lives in that field? (By the way I love her hoof trimmings the farrier leaves by the gate.) Ohhhh!

I looked at Ma, who looked back, shaking her head. "Brocky boy, that's just a fancy horse coat she wears every year. Silly Sealy." *Rude*, I thought but on closer inspection, yes, it was my friend's head poking out. Phew right. Such puzzling things in the world, like the time I got really excited when Ma said, "Let's go down to the zebra crossing," and all there was was stripes on the road 😵‍💫.

We crossed through the park which was empty. Lawks alive, and bury me bone, what has got into the woman? She made a beeline for the swings. On she clambered 😵. She sat on a swing, going backwards and forwards, no crash hat or elbow and knee protectors, nearly kicking me in the head as she came swooping down towards me. Luckily my lead was on full extension, or I would have been floored. Dear lord, has she lost it? Already worrying about what humans get called dementia. Anyway, after a while she staggered off, brushed herself down, and off I trotted, firmly attached to my Ma. It was straight home for her, showing me up like that. Good job none of my mates were around. Street cred would have been straight out of the window. Hope your day is better than mine. If I could blush with embarrassment, I would be a pink Sealy 🐼♡ .

11ᵗʰ September 2022

Monday smelly bin day. Ma's on the computer next door, so gone back to bed. This morning was lovely. Smelly walk around bins on pavement. Poked my nose round a garden wall as I do, and 👀 lawks alive, and bury me bone, nose to nose with a gigantic cat as big as a tiger spitting and growling. (Speak a little cat, and the language was dreadful.) Well, it was big anyway, so I just gave it a super-Sealy killer frown, flicked my ear back over my shoulder, and sauntered on. Ma was very surprised. See, can control myself sometimes.

The other day when it was really hot, I was taking Ma past a garden fence when I heard a gurgling noise. Looked up at Ma thinking, *Uh-uh,* but not her belly (thank goodness). Then came splashes and laughter and voices and a little girl squealing. Ma told me that they would be in something called a hot tub where people invite friends around and they all sit in the water together 👀. What? I shook my head. Unbelievable. When Auntie Pat comes around or anybody else, Ma doesn't say, "Let's go and fill the bath up and sit in it." Why would you do that? Rude. More polite to have a bath at your own home before you visit anybody. Humans have very strange habits. Think of nothing worse than to ask my mates round for a bath. I'd soon lose them pretty fast 🐼♡   .

12ᵗʰ September 2022

Well, interesting walk for me anyway. Got Ma leashed up and off. Hopefully she behaves today. First stop, charity shop in town. Allowed in there. Good sniff around; strictly no leg cocking 😗. On the way out, I got stopped. Yup, caught in the act: one fluffy slipper in my mouth. Had to give it back. Hmmmph. Thought it was a *charity* shop. Ma apologetic, but as I pointed out, why would you leave slippers on the floor at dog level? Ah well.

Around riverside walk saw a man crouching down by a mastiff. Dodgy, so Ma dragged me away, and I stopped and did a lot of back-leg scratching and kicking soil up high. I use my front paws too, so quite a lot of soil went flying, just to let him know not me that was worried but Ma. Then, how very interesting: Tesco delivery arrived to one of the houses across from our path. OK, call it a break, but settled down, lying there, watching every move. Food being taken in. I was in my element. driver and customer were very amused and laughing. Ma was not offered treats for me. Nope, not moving; ton weight at the end of her lead 😔. All done, delivered, so off I trotted.

Evil swan was there, the swanlets nearly as big as her—still brown, though. Much as I hate the evil birds, they are excellent ma's. On the way back along town walk, a man suddenly appeared out of the woods and crossed over the bridge. Not a word spoken. I gave him my super-Sealy killer frown. Just saying, I know most people, but not him. Stranger in our midst. Glad to see molehills are back. They must have returned from their holidays. Going to help Ma weeding the garden this afternoon. That will be fun. She will appreciate that 😋♡   🐼.

17th September 2022

Garagegate. Well, what a fun walk. Ma had forgotten it was garage sales day. Started right in my close with three stalls. Of course I had to inspect them and get petted by my neighbours and thanked for my watchdog duties (would there be a medal in this? got me wondering 🤔). I had to look at all the things on display (this was going to be a very long walk😵). Anyway, off I trotted with Ma in tow. Hats, shoes, clothes, and stuffed toys begging to be ripped apart (pictures not for me unless there were Sealy pics). Boxes and boxes of stuff just asking for a Brock spray, but told firmly nooo. Saw a really lovely hat with things dangling off it. Made a grab for it, but Ma was on the ball, especially after the slipper incident at the not so very charitable charity shop 😵. To crown it all, the Saturday cattle market was on too, so I took Ma past there so she could have some deep smells, as she loves the smell of cow pats. Embarrassing really, but I had had my smells so she deserved a little pleasure. Spread the Sealy love around today. Wonder I'm not bald, all the head rubs I've had. All in all, better than bin day—well, nearly. Chicken and kibble, here I come. Hope you have all had as good a Saturday as me. Must just say, Miss Ziggy Stardust couldn't wait to tell me she's a torty influencer now because of her fashion statement today with her purple petunia hat. Ma took a pic of her 🐢😵. Won't disillusion her dream on scaly girl 😅. (Love her, really; just banter) 🥰♡ 🐶.

23rd September 2022

Hi, there. Sorry about the drippy beard; just had a drink. Will wipe it later on the carpet 😅. Yesterday was a good walk. Spotted lots of elves in high-viz jackets in a crocodile—*what* 😳? Ma said that's what you call it when you walk in a line. They crossed the zebra crossing (all these animal names strange), and I pulled Ma to get a better look 👀. Ohhhh 😑 —disappointing. Not elves at all but very small people. There were normal size people with them anyway. Ma said they were from the nursery school. OK, one was in a pushchair, so attached myself to that for a while (not literally). and joined the crocodile. Wait till I tell my mates I was in a 🐊 crocodile and survived 🥰, and I walked over a 🦓 zebra.

All going well until we passed a child jail. Yes, we did. Screaming and running around, and one lad was climbing the gate, making a bid for freedom no doubt. I asked Ma to let them out. "Silly Brock!" Well, that was rude! "For starters they are schoolchildren, and it's their playtime." Well, they sounded like tortured souls. The screams—ummmmph. And Ma tells me off if I bark too much.

Next encounter was a fourteen-week-old miniature dachshund called Wilba. We had such a game. Cheeky upstart grabbed a mouthful of my beautiful beard. Lawks alive, and bury me bone, luckily for her she didn't pull any out. That would have been it. Sealies do not have lopsided beards. Quite an interesting walk, and Ma didn't pull; she behaved. Quite pleased she's coming along in leaps and bounds with my training. Didn't have to offer her any treats either (good thing; I'd eaten them all). 😅 Enjoy your weekend ♡ 🐶.

26th September 2022

Sometimes I am quite deaf. Think it's a male failing in humans too 😔. I have to have my daily roll; short one this morning. Met nice lady who said I walk with attitude 👀👀. Excuse me, who is this attitude I'm walking with? Invisible to my eyes. Maybe it's a pretend friend like little children have. OK, I'll roll with that (see what I did there 🤣 make myself laugh).

Anyway, Ma and I and attitude went past the children's prison again. They were running around and screaming behind those big iron padlocked gates. Then a prison guard came out and blew a whistle, and they all went running inside. Back to the cells, I suppose. Ma reminded me that it was called a school. Ummmph. Lawks alive, and bury me bone, can't believe they are there willingly. Going to start up a petition: free child prisoners. That will teach 'em 😋.

In the park playground the little people I thought were elves in their high-viz jackets were playing on the slides and roundabouts. I really wanted to join in but had to be content to stare through the railings. At one point the sky went as black as thunder. Ma just said thunder doesn't have a colour 🙂. Have to give her that, I suppose. Anyway it went dark, OK, Ma? Whatever. Having my cucumber treats now before morning nap 🤡♡

27th September 2022

Playground empty. Hmmmm; I wonder if I could sneak in and play on the slide🤪. "Of course not" Ma's retort. Well, this morning had Ma in a panic, out of bed, into the garden, and she heard me shrieking. Out she dashes. Yup, behind my shed, that cat that taunts me. I flushed it out. It flew over the fence after our birds; only I'm allowed to chase them. Ma hadn't heard my hunting call before the cheek of that cat.

Had a great rough and tumble with an American Labrador neighbour bigger than our Labs— huge. In fact, had to stand on tippy paws to reach his mouth. Great fun. I have developed a new post-poo dance. I call it the four-paw shuffle. Might be a trendsetter here. Not only do I send dirt and grass flying with my back paws, but I incorporate both front paws scratching. It does look quite fierce and very macho😈. Sometimes utter some grunts as well for effect.

Came home from paddock playschool this morning quite wet with dirtified paws. Lawks alive, and bury me bone, that got me under the hosepipe 👀. All that hard work undone. I'm now quite white and fluffy again. Can't do a thing with my beard or eyebrows, but did catch a glance—well, a long gaze to be honest in the garden mirror. Mmmmm, what a dashing Sealy looked back at me. Flicked the ear back, curled my tail as tight as it would go, and off I swaggered. Maybe being clean has its moments ♡   🤡.

1st October 2022

I'm not telling anyone that I was playing with a toy mouse up at Auntie Pat's yesterday. Yesterday was interesting. There were two small planes doing aerobatics, and Ma said they were having a "dogfight". Now more silly human talk. How can planes fight like us dogs? Well, obviously they can't, any more than we can do plane fights 😵.

Further on met a *huge* handsome (hurts to say it) dog. We got chatting, and turns out he's a visitor—only eleven months old, beagle-Labrador cross. Looked more like a heavy taller lurcher. Well, we played—a bit like playing with a horse 🐴. His name was Hank. I went on tippy paw and whispered in his ear, "Hi, I'm Brock, a super-Sealy. Rare breed, you know. And I would introduce you to my new invisible friend (they say I've got) if I could see him. His name is Attitude; doesn't roll off the tongue, does it? Actually don't see the point of him." Hank looked at me strangely, probably jealous cos he hasn't got one, and I trotted on with Ma and attitude in tow (I suppose).

Oh, next drama was a keeshond on the run, escaped from his house. Only a youngster. Lawks alive, and bury me bone, he was dancing around the traffic. Then his pa went walking after him, getting completely ignored as he was yelling and cursing 🤬. Left them to it; they were off at a speed. Now I've been told you can have a website or something and people pay to watch you eat 🙂. Asking Ma about setting me up for that. I could make sooo much money. I could buy myself a red super-Sealy cape. Mind you, probably be so fat I wouldn't get off the ground 🐶🤭😂.

Cattle market day. Lovely smells; Ma's favourite is cow pats 😍😍. Each to their own (takes her back to Wales when she was little). Interesting sniffs on the tyres of the Land Rovers and trucks; shame I can't roll on them. Back now for coffee and cucumber 🥒. Love cucumber. Like a sliver of carrot too but only if it's delicately pared. Upsetting morning, as my routine went all to pot. Ma had to go for flu and Covid jabs early before our walk, so looking forward to what's now my brunch. Happy weekend. Uh-uh, Ma's just said I've written too much, and people will be nodding off halfway through. Rude, I thought. Have faith, Ma ♡ ♡ 🐶.

2nd October 2022

Beardgate. What do I look like? Nasty shock after walk this afternoon. Straight out of the back door, saw the bowl of water and shampoo and that wicked black snake thing that spits water at me. And my old playpen cutting off any escape. Now got a pristine clean beard. Really upsetting, as I had cultivated the smell of pilchards in tomato sauce (although that's drained off; got to watch the waistline). My beard had a reddish hue, which I thought very Jack the Lad. Don't know why Ma bothered with a towel, as I carpet-surfed myself dry.

I do enjoy peeping under fences and under garden gates on our walks. Ma says it's rude and I will be called a voyeur 👀. Thought that sounded very classy and French, so happy with that. I was accused by Ma of having ADHD. Now that sounds fantastic; maybe even get a medal from King Charles the third 👑 for it. I can be needy, I know. Every morning, if Ma doesn't put our phone, her newspaper, and a cup of tea on our settee arm, I will let her know, talking at her till she does. But who doesn't like love attention and routine—oh, and their own way 🐶😍?

Pilchards finished now, so must be careful how I eat my meat topper on my kibble (special kibble with calming properties 🙂; doesn't work 🤪) to keep my beard clean. Enjoy your evening 🐶♡ .

3rd October 2022

Look through the door. I think that could be my invisible friend Attitude. Sure looks like a Sealy. Maybe I have had him all my life and didn't know. It looks like the guy in the oven and garden mirrors and in our little woodstove thingy. Just shows how clever he is; only shows up in glass. Stayed a long time reacquainting myself with him. He didn't say a woof to me, but probably invisible friends don't talk ♡ 🐶.

4th October 2022

Well, here we are, doing the river walk under the willows. Very picturesque, must say. But bin day today, so missing out doing my "hunter-gathering"—mopping up rubbish dropped 😣. Still, lots of animal smells here I expect my friend Attitude is here somewhere. If I could see him, I could maybe nudge him into the river, and that would be that.

Ma had her flu and Covid jabs on Saturday in the same arm, so she could keep her right arm Sealy friendly. I can pull her along if needs be. It's a week since she had her cataract surgery, and luckily her eye didn't drop out or anything. Didn't fancy picking up a squashy eye 👁 so now she can see me with both 👀 and no glasses, which is very sad for me. I loved glasses snatching. I had perfected the art. But of course I'm a bit older now and concentrate on getting all the insoles out of her boots, shoes, you name it, I'll do it. Perfectionist at heart.

Very excited, as going to Sealy meet-up with Eddie and Buffy. East Midlands/Cambridgeshire Meet-Up on Saturday. Hope it's a nice autumn day, and I am the named navigator for Ma 😂😂😂. Hopefully she remembers from last time. Enjoy the rest of your day 🐶♡   .

6ᵗʰ October 2022

Well, even I have to admit "bad bad boy" was apt. not that I heard it through the red mist that had developed over my eyes😾🐾. My nemesis was across the road—lawks alive, and bury me bone. I alerted the whole neighbourhood just as Ma was talking to a friend, saying she'd never had such an affectionate boy 😂🤭. Wheee! Lead lunge, harness straining, Ma holding on with both hands, gripping the pavement with her size sevens—well, of course she was soo embarrassed after singing my praises. My halo landed right down on that pavement. The friend said, "I'll leave you to it" 😂and left us. Ma said it was like trying to land a whale. The lead was turning round and round, nearly wriggled out of my harness twisting and turning (that's why I also wear a collar—belt and braces). Kept it up till the spotted creature disappeared. Ummmph; fine start to the walk. Ma not happy even when I looked up with a grin, tongue hanging out—that was disrespectful too, I was told. 😵 Should be ashamed of myself apparently. Where, I'd like to know, was my supposed wingman Attitude? Invisible as usual.

The rest of the walk was better. Played with two lovely little Yorkies. the girl flirted outrageously with me, and, being polite, I responded, sniffing her as expected of a healthy Sealy, posturing, flicking my ear over my back before flinging myself on my back with legs kicking and tongue out. Got quite a few treats from their dad, so did Sealy commando crawl for him as an extra.

Met Helen, Sue, and Millie. Helen and Sue are humans and sisters, and Millie is a pretty spaniel. Got big fuss from them. Sue said she liked my posts, so did something right on this walk. Off now; chastened, but not that chastened. Wait till I see that darn Dalmatian again. Thing is, and here's the real annoying thing, he doesn't even look at me 🐾. Wonder if he's deaf, and I'm wasting my breath 😜🐶♡   . Ma's groomer came, Tammy. Ma seems to enjoy being groomed. Doesn't mind the hair dryer. A bit weird, methinks ♡   .

9ᵗʰ October 2022

Well, what an exciting social weekend. My social secretary (Ma) had a job keeping my diary up to date. Yesterday was our Cambs and East Midlands Meet-Up for Sealies. My Auntie Jenny came too, as she loves me and dogs. Great day. Wow. I slept like a log; so did Ma last night. Ma's son coming over this morning. The car drew up 😲. Ma's great granddaughter Fiadh and her ma and her pa *and* the jam on the buttie, George, my big mate who is their Labrador, climbed out with Ma's son. I'm his shadow. I love Adrian. Didn't know what to do with myself, sooo excited, and of course, where baby Fiadh goes, so do food and dropped bits. George proceeded to loot my toys, but I don't mind, as we are mates since I was a young pup. Had a power struggle to get on Adrian's knees. Fiadh was there, but she just giggled. My invisible friend Attitude sulked in a corner cos he wasn't the centre of attention, I imagine—as he didn't seem to be there. Wouldn't have known anyway if he's invisible, would I 🤭? How we managed two walks as well, lawks alive, and bury me bone, it beats me. Looking forward to my dinner and another snooze. Hope you have all had a good weekend 🤡♡ .

11ᵗʰ October 2022

Happy Sealy sunny Sunday. It was lovely; had to chase the aliens from top of the wall first, then off we trotted. Millions of people about. OK, it was busy 😊. Ma's peeping over my shoulder again. There were people riding chariots on the path; I nearly got mowed down. Hmmph. Saw a man pushing a chair on wheels. The lady sitting in it had a little cheewahwah beside her, and it snarled at me. Gave it my super-Sealy death frown, swished my tail, and sashayed by 😊. Ma's just corrected me *again*. Not chariots; mobility scooters. Not a chair on wheels, it's called a wheelchair. And misspelt *cheewahwah* 😊. The way she goes on, I will give up and let her write it down herself. Grrrrrr. We passed lots of people drinking outside a big house. I wanted to go there too, but oh no, didn't happen. Then up the hill and more laughter coming from a door of a big house. Wanted to go in there too; again, oh no. My sunny Sunday is clouding over; a lot of *no*'s going on.

Walking down a country road, and the smells coming from a ploughed field on my right were just too much. Had my head stuck in every gap. You guessed it—another *no*. Well, got to the gate, and I did a really big Houdini wriggle trying to get out of my harness. Stamped my paw and gave it my best Sealy shriek. Some people passing by thought that was really funny, so I did an encore 🤡🤡🤡. Ma was very underwhelmed by the whole performance and gave a weak smile at them and made some excuse, humiliating me. Really? I'd put on a grand performance. Got to the sailing club then. Lawks alive, people all over the water on paddle boards, yachts, and canoes. I was told firmly dogs are not allowed to be sea cadets 😇. Lawks alive, it looked such good fun.

When I got home, I was ready for a meal and a big snooze and dreamt of drinking in a garden, going to the house of laughter, and running around the ploughed field. Lastly I had a sea cadet's hat on my head, and I was on the prow of a yacht, wind blowing through my beard. Of course I was the captain, and the crew called me an old sea dog (less of the old).

11th October 2022, continued …

Hedgehog *mine*! Shuffle round of Ma's toys (she calls it a doorstop) 😖. She put it in the wrong place. I was there in a flash, and off we went. I think I can hear Ma saying something, but can't quite catch it. Anyway, Attitude put me up for this. He has his uses, even if nobody can see him. Eventually hedgehog retrieved, a bit wet and slightly mouthed 😁.

This morning Paddock playschool, then home. Bored, as Ma was doing something called cleaning (👀that's a novelty😁). The spiders evacuated their hammocks, swinging away in their webs cocktails down, sunglasses off, and scuttled away to a new location (they'll probably be fine for another six months). Since she's had her other cataract done, she can actually see what needs to be done. Hoping this novelty will wear off, as I hate that machine that sucks up all the crumbs I was saving for emergencies. Disgraceful. Obviously my needs are not being met. Well, I've made my feelings clear, so Ma is going to let me take her for a walk now. So chin-chin, my friends 🐶♡   .

13th October 2022

Good boy 😇. Ma's not been well. Some bug that's going around, and very small walk yesterday. Early to our bed (fine by me, the bed bit, that is). Well, halo round my paws today. A Sealy can only last haloed for a short time. Back to neighbourhood watch duty. A passer-by could be a potential dog snatcher. Who knows? Better safe than sorry.

Then when Ma's groomer was here, Ma heard strange noises from the garden, so mid hair blow-dry, Sealyhamy investigation party came charging out. I looked up: black beard, leaves on head, tongue hanging out—looking very pleased with myself. The garden is completely patioed, but found the one place under the little sun house thingy where there were large pebbles over a skin, usually barricaded off with flower pots. (Yeah, well, done me😂). Ground skin ripped, and there I struck gold. Well, soil, really, and I got stuck in it. Hence Brock Blackbeard: very filthified. You guessed it, barriers back in place 😠. Hope you all have a good evening ♡   🐶.

15th October 2022

Well, when I did wake up or rather *got* woken up, off we trotted. Hitched Ma up to my lead; onwards and upwards. Met my new neighbours yesterday, Sue and her husband, but guess what their surname is. It's Elite. Now they must be very special to have a name like that, so from now on, to me they will be known as the Elites (the special very important neighbours). I had my ears tickled and big fuss made of me, so did my commando crawl for them. Today it was rain, sun, and continual wind (the weather, not Ma 😤; darnt say other 😆), and we saw a muntjac deer and her baby deerlet—Ma's butting in. *Yes, I know it's not called that.* Really, to me it's a deerlet, so be it honestly 😑. *Antiques Road Trip* last night on the picture box they were at Sealyham in Wales, from whence we came, and the big house you see, I felt it in my bones. We were bred as "killing machines". Well, I'm not going to remind anybody about the fledgling I had in my mouth 😕😫 in the spring. It wriggled and squirmed, clawing away, and tasted foul. That's why I spat it out—the one that got away. Why would I want to kill anything (apart from my nemesis Dalmatian spotty thing)? Rabbits are a valuable source of Maltesers, so they are off my kill list for sure. Maybe I haven't got the "kill gene"; might need training session with the SAS if that's required of me. Lawks alive, and bury me bone, why would I want to be any different? Couch potato, spoilt rotten, treats, fed well, allowed to take Ma out twice a day. Naahhh, can't be bothered. I even let Ma share my bed, and I've had all new warm sheets and duvet covers bought for me, and we have a large electric blanket, too. Mmmm, no. Stay as I am, thank you very much 🤡♡   .

15th October 2022, continued …

Being on Sealy high alert, I can see you but you can't see me 😂🤡♡.

17ᵗʰ October 2022

Just checking the post. Regular postie Debbie posts a gravy bone for me her day off, so no treat. No post either. Like to open and read Ma's post. Good job Ma likes doing jigsaw puzzles 😂😂🤡♡   .

19ᵗʰ October 2022

Well, look at me. My best friend Jane was walking the Samoyeds, as she is a "professional dog walker"; don't you know. See, I have proper titled friends 😍 but that was this afternoon. This morning very important and eventful for me. There was that great out-of-space machine that stalks me (they don't think I know), lights flashing, rumbling along, brushing all my tasty bits out of the road. I gave it my super-Sealy killer frown, and on we went, but wow wow wow, what on earth is that?

A very hairy rat was running on the fence top. Lawks alive, off we went. Ma didn't have much choice 🙄🐿. I chased it up a tree and spent ages sniffing its trail. Oh, here she comes. I have to tell you, hairy rat was called a squirrel. Well, how did I know that 😵? Some people have a chip on their shoulder; I have Ma. Anyway, that was this morning. This afternoon I had a game with a lovely spaniel. Then, oh my beating heart, a white truck thing passed me. Ohhhh, the smell delicious, so I dragged Ma after it. It stopped right by me. I had to lie down and watch two nice men who made a fuss of me, and then they emptied the dog poo bin. Lush smell. I was lucky enough to meet them at another bin. Then of course my Samoyed friends came along. I'm an honorary member of the pack 😃😃😆😆. So good day so far; sleeping it all off now, chasing great hairy rats 😃😴.

20th October 2022

Well, where to start. Woken up early morning, thunder, lightning ⚡. Then woke up 8.45 👀. Yes, we overslept. Thunderous rainstorm. Ma was up first, it was so dark. Then she dragged me off our bed 😔. "Come on, Brocky boy, up and at 'em." Ummm, don't think so, Ma. It's pouring. Well, I got fooled. Back door open, Ma shouting "Get out, cats!" Clapping her hands like someone possessed. Shot out back: inspection of boundary's complete. Of course, cats hate rain. Back in; won't get caught again.

Walkies. Had had my mackerel on kibble brekkie, but don't think I will see many folk to give fishy kisses to today. Once out, Ma believes wet is wet, may as well plod on. I had my grassy roll as usual, but managed to roll on soil as well. *Filthified*. Yeah, brown back and neck. All Susie's (my beautician) work on Monday down the chute 😖. Embarrassing. The wetter I got, the more my black Sealy spots all over my body came to the fore 😎. Don't mind, but it makes me look more like a version of my nemesis (the dreaded Dalmatian).

I saw a picture of a police dog with new helmet with cameras. Well, I've got serious helmet envy. Asked Ma, "Perleese can I have one for Xmas? I could wear it while on neighbourhood watch duties from the back of my settee." Well, it's going to be a very. boring day. Not many folk out there to monitor. Going to have a damp snooze now. Ciao for now (yes, I'm learning Italian). Arrivederci ♡   🐶. Spaghetti. Just added that 😹.

21ˢᵗ October 2022

Hi, guys. Sunny cold walks today. This afternoon I saw an excellent specimen for my museum of corpses: a squashed pigeon. *No*, I was told very firmly and was also informed that I was to drop this hobby. Said I would 😬. Will still be on the lookout though—people stuff animals, so can't see Ma's problem. Then I found this grand stick which I dragged around with me, but not allowed to bring it indoors. Life can be very trying when I can't get my own way 🙁🐾🐶.

21ˢᵗ October 2022, continued …

Ma said it was raining cats and dogs 🙀. Luckily they missed us cos I didn't see any. Would hate to have them land on my head. Unbelievable (very, but that's Ma for you—things she comes out with). Out we trotted. Slight shower, then boom 😳. Down it came. Cloudburst bouncing off the ground, Did a quick Sealy trot home out in full view. My black Sealy spots started to show. (Must say I have a beautiful pattern of them round my derriere. See, I told you I was learning French.) Gave the hall a good spattering before I dived onto my towel, ready on the floor for me, followed up by carpet surfing and sofa surfing. All in all, everything is damp 🫠. Lawks alive, and bury me bone, *rude*. Ma is only lighting incense sticks now as she said the house smells of wet dog 😵. Good job I'm thick-skinned. She should think herself lucky I don't smell of cats dry or wet 😹♡   🐶.

22ⁿᵈ October 2022

What a day. *Dry*, at least. I was getting "paw rot". Went for lovely long road walk to make up for yesterday. Took us ages, as people were making a fuss of me. (Love it; flutter my eyelashes, quite long under the eyebrows, and cuddle up to them.) 🫠🫠 Hooray. What do I see but a red postal cart coming my way. My fave postie, Debbie, was on duty, so treats, high-fiving as though my life depended on it.

Further on saw a very dead mouse untouched by feline fangs by the looks of it 😄. Now is it any good trying to get Ma to reinstate my corpse museum? *No*. Leave it was the answer to that! 🙁 Then I had a thought. A dead mouse? Lawks alive, and bury me bone, I had recently seen on the picture box a program about *the plague*. Realize it was rats, *but* may be the start of a mini plague. Must look out for more mice that just drop down dead unmarked and secrete them in my beard to take home and do an autopsy by mouth of course and be world-famous. Be on the picture box even. Be the first Sealy scientist. Well, off for last trundle round the block before dinner, of course keeping an eye out for corpses 🤡♡ . I know Ma says I live in my own dream world (prefer horror film—more exciting 😹).

24ᵗʰ October 2022

Well, lovely afternoon walk. Ma took me down some new places and smells. I couldn't believe my luck (see pic). A beautiful dirty old work boot—oh joy 😻. Managed to get my head right in before I was yanked away. What a fragrance; heavenly. Pleaded to bring it home. Well, you can guess the answer to that 😖. Got the same reaction to my museum of corpses. Ma's not got much imagination.

A lovely man made such a fuss of me and then thanked Ma. What about me? It was me he stroked 😽. Then on the way home I met my pug mates Dylan and Boris. Dylan, who is nearer to me in the pic, sang me a snatch from some opera. Ohhhh, that boy can howl. It was quite a long aria. I wonder if he can do ballet as well, as he seems very educated. So home for chicken and kibble with cucumber 🥒 treats while Ma has her kibble, although it looks better than mine. I shall dream of singing and dancing tonight 😴, though I refuse to wear tights. xx

25th October 2022

Got to go to doctor's this afternoon as I keep scratching my ear 🫨. I expect the dreading weighing in (more treat deprivation coming; feel it in my bones) that you have to do every visit. Love going to the doctor's. (Ma said I'm lucky, as easier to see my doc than hers. In fact, she's thinking of signing on with my doc 🐶.) I'm fine until they want to stand me on that table, and I clench my ample buttocks, not knowing which end those gloved hands are going. Keep you posted 🐶🖤   .

25th October 2022, continued …

Well, back from the doc's. Think he was a wizard cos he wore little specs and had a pointy white beard. Of course I hadn't scratched my ears once since Ma had made my appointment 🐶🫨. Ma knew really nowt wrong, as pink, non-smelly ears. (In the past Ma said, if her Scottie had bad ears, other dogs would make a beeline to smell them.) And £80 later (mind you, did have injection and tabs to take) off we trotted. Ma feels better now too, as she's had me checked. Had a struggle to get me past big white van, as I stood firmly planted, nose twitching. Of course Ma said he's having his lunch. How mean, never even shared it, but I did a very swift sarnie snatch (sarnie, Scouse for sandwich) off the pavement, even though Ma slammed her size sevens over it 😂. As soon as I got to my surgery, I jumped on the scales as is expected of me. Fully dressed, of course. I reckon my collar and harness weigh at least four kilos 🐶. Now 15.7 kilos; was 15.9, so lost a bit of weight I never even batted an eyelash as I had my injection. That's how brave and courageous I am. Mind you, the wizard never went near my nether regions. Knew I was fairly safe as he didn't have the dreaded rubber gloves on. Dinner time now, so leave you all to have yours 🐶♡   .

29th October 2022

"Fungal morning"—that's what Ma calls this weather (worked at the vet's and the doctor's too long, methinks). Warm, moist, and damp. There are lots of 🍄 springing up from the grass. Give her the benefit of the doubt 🫨. Funny old walk; soo many peemails to decipher. Lots of concerns in the canine world. Are we being overrun by pesky cats 😝? also pressing canine world matters to sort out. Met lovely lady in a chariot who stopped and made a fuss of me. Crossed the road at the traffic lights when the bleepers started. To my delight a shiny packet opened on the pavement half full of cheese pie. Well, we both made a dive for it (didn't realize Ma was so hungry). Guess who won🐶.

Well, safely over the road there ensued a very ungainly tussle. Yup, actually I'd call it assault, and by my own Ma. Lawks alive, and bury me bone, what's the world coming to? (Half a mind to call the legals. My pals across the pond have contacts.) Tug of war ensued, teeth firmly gripping (mine, by the way) and occasionally a quick gobble. It was quite wet from the rain. My beard got pulled ☹️   . Ma hooked some squelchy stuff out of the side of my mouth, flicking it onto the pavement, but in a feeding frenzy I was trying to eat the wrapper too. So tug of war with that as well. Wonder we didn't both end up rolling around on the ground. *Rude* I call it, making a show of me like that. Eventually fight over, and Ma had to walk home holding the lead with a squashy, mucky hand. Smelly too😷. Think I won. Certainly had some of that delicious soggy pie. Can't wait to see what our afternoon walk will bring. Not much, I expect; only short one, as main one in the morning. Don't forget to put the clocks back. Not sure what Ma means. Back to where 🤕🤔? Nowt so queer as folk 😵. Ah well. Happy weekend 🤡♡   .

1ˢᵗ November 2022

Foxgate🐾🐾🐾🐾. Just back from paddock playschool and *yes*, found the elusive fox pooh. Beginning to think it didn't exist. Well that was so good, did a head dive and a Sealy roll onto my back. What happened when I got home so proud? Mmmmm, unforgivable. Dragged to cordoned-off part of garden, spitty black snake thing was turned on, Ma drenched me, soapy stuff all over me, and I ended up screaming. Yup, I did, loud and clear, so waiting for the knock on the door from the legals or RSPCA or police. I really laid it on. If Ma gives me lots of treats, might drop the charges 🤕. Wondering if fox pooh is worth it, as I didn't have the beautiful aroma for long. Howleen was a downer too. I wanted to go trick-or-treating, but Ma's ample size seven squashed that as well. So going to water any leftover evil orange things I see on my next walk. Ma not in my good books at the moment. "As damp as a damp squib" (another weird saying humans come up with 😵), even after carpet surfing and over-vigorous rub-down by Ma. Least now I can say *I've done it*—baptism by fox pooh. My initiation as a fully fledged member of the fox pooh rollers is complete. Attitude, my invisible friend, didn't get a look in 😂🤡♥   .

A scary pumpkin left over from Halloween

5ᵗʰ November 2022

Flash-bang, flash-bang. Ma said it's bonfire night. Not bothered in the slightest, which is really odd, as slightest noise outside usually starts off a Sealy rallying call. Saw a white ghost cat

Howleen night creeping around, staring, probably casting an evil spell on me. Ma said it might be deaf, as some all-white animals are. There you go; that's why I have selective hearing when Ma calls me. (I have patches of lemony brown on my head and ears faded from tan.) Yesterday a passer-by called me a stubborn Westie, as I wouldn't move from reading a peemail 😵. Westie😞 . Soon got put right.

Went visiting yesterday. Met up with Ma's groomer, Tammy, and her two little dogs. Went to see her brother. Well, he thought I was a grand boy. I had the run of his house and garden, and he was clapping his hands, egging me on. Should be more people like him. I got very excited. Ma's been a real drag; dreadful walks. she just wouldn't come the way I wanted her to. Very stubborn. (Well, she's half Welsh; stubborn streak runs in the Welsh). I was digging all four paws firmly on the ground, then lying down and threw a bit of commando crawling in for good measure; anything to jolly her on 😸. Stay safe, and don't be frightened of the flash-bangs 🐶♡ .

6th November 2022

Like walking through town as I try to go in all the shops and pubs, and maybe, just maybe, food on the ground. Still ravenous even though steroids nearly over. Went through a place called a cemetery, and Ma said best behaviour—no watering *anything*. Had a sit-down on a lady's chariot. She liked that; I got lots of strokes. I fancy going to these prisons (although they look like big houses). To make older people happy, I'd commando crawl, Sealy-sit, and make funny sounds. Can do a mean yodel and a four-paw shuffle. (Unicycle riding not perfected yet and very uncomfortable 😵.) Ma said good idea, but emphatically *no*. Rude. I thought she said didn't think they'd like to be jumped on, and with them not being so quick, having the food whipped out of their hands. So that was short-lived.

Toilet paper chase yesterday. Don't know what came over me (blamed my invisible friend Attitude). Down the stairs and round the living room 😂. Ma not amused well it was only one roll dyekgftyyjn, —Sorry about that. Just flung phone across the room. Debbie postie coming to our door, which means my posted treat will be on the doormat. My eyebrows are getting so long, nearly like a Sealy fall hairdo. OK when I'm walking into the wind, and very effective when I toss my head in the air when I'm strutting my stuff. Thinking plaits, but groomer's soon. Ummmm, another of my ideas dashed into the ground. Happy Thursday, folks.

7th November 2022

Well, fed up of getting wet, drying out, only to get wet again. Yesterday Auntie Pat came down to have some medicine with Ma 😹. They seem to enjoy it. Makes them laugh, soooo when they were dosing themselves up I snook out. Uh-uh. Ma said, "Brock's quiet (a quiet Sealy is up to no good). Just check on him." There I stood in the hall surrounded by shredded tissue and a sweet. Auntie Pat's coat had been put on the bannisters. Had to balance on the bottom stair, but managed to empty her coat pocket, leaving a sloppy wet pocket. Little did they know until Auntie Pat was going home and met a doggy friend and went to get a biscuit out of her pocket 😊   😂. It was empty. I had eaten all the biscuits. Good bit of thievery there. Blamed my imaginary friend Attitude. He makes me do such dreadful things 😹😹. That will teach Ma to keep her eye on me when entertaining. They should have known as soon as A.P. arrived. My head dived straight in her bag, and I ran off with her hat, which I exchanged for a sliver of extra mature cheddar. Method in my madness 😂. I will drop anything from my mouth for cheese.

13th November 2022

Adoration. My Ma's son Adrian came to visit. This man brought Ma to pick me up, so of course I love him very much, and I am his shadow whenever he comes. His wife Lon is lovely too; just that I can't get enough of Adrian, which she is quite happy about 😅. Well, murky misty start to our day. Ma behaved quite well, though had to drag her past cats. Getting better (it was me really getting dragged past cats, did you guess?). I actually chose our route, and she didn't play up (for once). Think I'm getting her trained at last.

After yesterday's beard washing trauma. (Still debating getting my new legals based in Wales: Tedimus H Bailey. John Edward Herman, the Dobermann, has been assigned to me. expert cut-throat legal speciality to the stars, divorces, and Sealies. He's merciless.) I was plonked on

Adrian's knees, and Ma descended on me, brandishing a comb and brush, firmly gripping my head and attacking my beard with said weapons. She's really pushing it. Careful, Ma, just saying 😖. Lawks alive, and bury me bone, enough is enough! I won't take it any further if I can have extra treats every night and not see a brush or a comb for at least one month. Also I want to grow my hair and have dreadlocks; easier to keep clean (like a bit of reggae, me). I could be an inflewencer, start new hairstyles for Sealies. Enjoy your day, one and all ♡ 🐼.

15ᵗʰ November 2022

Well, guys, here you are witnessing a knighthood right here in my very own "hood". (Don't forget I'm Magical Duke, kennel name as well!) Young Frank performed the honours. Ted, the elder chap, watched on. Also little adopted girl. She's a little sweety hidden behind long hairy legs (dogs', not humans') 😂. Yup, we took up the whole pavement while the ceremony took place. Frank is about my age. They are both Spinone Italiano, so probably I'm an Italian knight. It was a very solemn affair, and afterwards I had to do the customary inspection of Frank's bits 😳. Well, it is expected of us; rude not to. The humans looked on, bemused, as you can see from Frank's expression. It was my duty as a Sealy knight to thoroughly check him out. My invisible friend Attitude will be sick as a pig with envy, and what a tale for Miss Ziggy Stardust 🦔 when she comes out of hibernation. (Lawks alive, and bury me bone, hibernation—pfhhht. Just an excuse for a long lay-in, I think).

I wonder if Frank and Ted would like to be honorary members of my "pug boy gang". We'd certainly be an awesome sight, dontcha think? Of course I've got to be De Capo, as it was my idea. We could go cat hunting—ah and hairy rats (spotted jumping around in the trees yesterday), and we could scare the living bejabers out of my nemesis, "Spotted Dick". Nooo, it's a fine nickname. As Ma said, there's a pudding called that, so not rude 😂😂😂😂. I just like writing it down. Abandoned after paddock playschool this morning soaking wet and filthified. Very pleased with myself. Dried myself off, and Ma went out with Auntie Pat hunter-gathering, she called it. Hah think not unless you call clothes shopping that. Not a treat in sight, but plenty of carrier bags when she came back home. My knighthood made up for everything, though Ma will have to curtsy now. (Hope the old gal doesn't lose her balance 😂). I will expect to be called upon for civil duties and guest appearances. (not letting this go to my head of course, but a knight has to do what a knight has to do.) Enjoy your evening, guys 🐼♡ . Knight Brock Hilditch Magical Duke to boot.

17ᵗʰ November 2022

Barrel-chested rude 🙁 , and Emily was my favourite vet. Went for my check-up and vaccs. Weigh 15.8 kg from 15.4, but still okay. She did add I was solid 💪 muscled. (Maybe I'm a giant Sealyham. Schnauzers have giants 👀.) Anyway, love going to the vets, but ohhhhh, that table— hate being on it. Kennel cough vacc—well, much to my shame, had to be taken out to have that done. Left Ma behind, and came sauntering in, job done, tossing my head. Attitude slinking in by my side; he was as much use as a chocolate teapot. Where's my patient's confidentiality, I ask myself. Lawks alive, and bury me bone, may as well have consultation in the high street. Just as well not got any embarrassing conditions.

Pouring with rain all day so time to think about my motto all knights have a motto now I've translated this from Latin (not everyone understands Latin). Here it is: Every Dog Has Its Day 🐶🐶. Now Ma says I've pinched that as a very old saying, but pshhh, don't care. Coat of arms, or as Eddie reminded me, coat of legs comes next. Ma went out yesterday for lunch with friend used to work with—got treated! Doggy bag non-existent on her return. There you go: guarded the house and everything, warning off intruders, with no reward. Story of my life.

Heard a strange expression today. Cats have nine lives. What the heck? Why should they have that many lives? What about us dogs? 😵 No justice 🐶♡ .

18ᵗʰ November 2022

Well, here is a picture of my coat of arms/legs. It's an actual one. Ma didn't even know she had one, so of course must stick with this. I was being a Womble this morning (again) picking up rubbish an empty sandwich wrapper lots of building going on, and workmen not very tidy after they've eaten their lunch. Not complaining 😆. Well, oh dear, what can I say? Ma arrived home after a hunter-gatherer trip with a hideous high-viz coat. She chased me round the house before cornering me, pouncing on me, and putting me in that hideous thing. Knights should have armour, shiny and becoming to one's standing, not a cheap, nasty thing like that. Been reassured, wear only if lots of rain. Mmmmm, lawks alive, and bury me bone. Very pleased with my coat of arms.

19ᵗʰ November 2022

Well, looky here. Market day. Transfixed by the magnificent sight and smell of this tractor's steps. Bliss, but no. Not allowed nearer. Wouldn't you know? Went a very wet walk (dry at the start, so escaped having to wear that appalling coat Ma bought me yesterday). She was dry in her Regatta coat she got herself yesterday. Rest assured, better quality than mine 😞 and a hundred pounds, knocked down from 340—black Friday sale, whatever that might be.

She was happy, as dry as a bone, whilst me very wet. Black spots threatening to show through, so I made Ma walk fast home. Street cred at risk; long walk as well. In disgrace, at the beginning of the walk, went right up to a border terrier and hurled stream of Welsh insults at his face. Clash of clans—well, that's my excuse also. Attitude told me to do it, sooo duty-bound. Ma mortified 😹, Every other dog got on fine with. We went on the walk with one of Ma's friends, Elaine, and her Jack Russell terrier, who keeps to herself, although she looked disgusted at me sniffing that beautiful farm dirt on the tractor. Probably jealous, truth be known 😹. Afternoon walk; bet I'll have to wear that coat. Happy wet Saturday, one and all ♡ 🐸🐾 .

20ᵗʰ November 2022

Just waiting for something to happen. Well, Miss Ziggy Stardust 🐢 has been brought out from her hibernation. That was short-lived. Ummmmph; back to hurl insults at me when Ma's not around. And she was sooo rude when I told her she'd have to curtsy to me, as I'm a knight now. She just sort of snorted and buried herself in the soil. Jealous, I suppose.

Well, not a nice Sunday walk this morning. That horrid black-and-white cat outside my door, so had to scream and curse that. Dancing around and pulling Ma about. Then I tried to snatch bread from the grass (birds dropped it?). I then insulted a cockapoo, barking in its face. Ma said I'm getting too big for my boots since being knighted 🥴🥴🥴. Boots? What boots? Please, she's not getting me high-viz boots to go with that hideous high-viz coat she bought me. I'm going on strike if she does. Did a fair bit of commando crawling this morning, every time she strayed from my chosen route. Well, it is my walk! Going to have to get her a leash that goes around her nose. Horrible but necessary if she doesn't improve. At least dry today. Beauty parlour tomorrow 😎. Get rid of any nice smells I've been able to get in my coat. Ah well, start from scratch again tomorrow. Life's tough 🐸♡   .

21ˢᵗ November 2022

Well, it's pouring with rain 🐾   all day, and I know, just know that high-viz abomination of a coat will eventually be worn for my afternoon walk. Miss Ziggy Stardust 🐢 (Right Honourable, as she's insisting on being called since my knighthood) has had a soak in her bath and promptly disappeared under her soil heat lamp—it's on but our heating is not 😵 If I could fit in her run, I'd lie under her lamp. Great. She has heat. We don't not until tonight, for couple of measly hours. Favouritism, methinks.

Not many passers by today. Not even ducks waddling by down the rivers of water (we live at the top of a hill, so water rushes down the road). Ma bought something called broccoli for me (spat it out last time), so she laced it with peanut butter just a bit 🤢. Spat that out too. I'll stick to cucumber and carrot shavings. Well, at least filthifying will happen on my walk. Job done 😹. Can't wait much longer for rain to stop, so Ma said let's bite the bullet 😳😳. What the heck? Lawks alive, and bury me bone, she does say some very weird things. She can bite whatever she likes. I'll stick to bones, thank you.

Well, here goes my hairstyle, and my straightened leg hair curls a-coming back with the wet. Off we trot. Bye for now, Brock Magical Duke Knight of the Realm mgrtys19r5tu jii, —Sorry about that Ma snatched my phone off me. Told me, "Get your paws down to earth, young man."

😳😳😳 There she goes again. Where else would my paws be, sky-walking? Ummmph. Think maybe they're all jealous of my titles 🐶♡   .

21st November, continued …

Well, do I look happy? ☹   Suppose Ma's satisfied now (actually fleecy lined and kept my back dry). Never walked so fast in all my life. No commando crawling out there today. Pouring down. I nearly aquaplaned a couple of times. Concerned re Ma. She can't swim (kept that quiet). Just going to put water wings on her if it gets any wetter. Won't we look a fine pair when we go round the lake and by the river, her in water wings with the leash around her nose (unless she becomes more obedient)? Can't keep giving her treats to walk better. She'll explode, and have to tell people, "Please don't feed Ma with treats. She's on a diet." Well. pilchards and kibble dinner soon 😊😊♡   🐶.

25th November 2022

Dummygate 🐾🐾. Fiadh, Ma's great granddaughter, came visiting. She wasn't crawling last time I saw her. I washed her face really well and tried to be gentle. (Hard for me—bull in a china shop, says Ma. Another weird expression. Do I have horns? *No*, I don't.) Success. She dropped her dummy, and off I went at the speed of light. Had dummy envy as soon as I saw it when she arrived, so result. Charged upstairs with Ma in hot pursuit, waving the extra strong cheddar cheese, shouting *"Cheese!"* at the top of her voice. Did the exchange on the landing. Then came the sterilisation part, which took ages. Boiling kettles, scrubbing dummy 😳 —*rude*, dontcha think? My tongue is in pristine condition, and I was courteous enough to have a drink washing my tongue before washing Fiadh's face and hijacking her dummy. (Well, let's face it. You don't want to know where my tongue had been 😷.) It was all very exciting especially the bit where Fiadh and I were sitting on Adrian's knee 😄 jostling for position. Megan (little elf's ma) was giving her some goodies to eat, so I sat as close as I could, Sealy superstare burning into their faces, even managing to drool and yep got a bit too 😋. Success again. Megan gave Ma a new dirt-sucking machine called Dyson. Now that was the only down bit of the visit. Ma of course thrilled to bits. Really thought when our Dyson thing had heart attack and went over the rainbow 🌈 bridge yesterday that I was rid forever, and I would have a Dyson-free life. Not so. Anyway hope you all have a good day, and Happy Thanksgiving Day to my pals across the pond. Can't wait to have more elf play 🦴😋🐶♡   .

27th November 2022

Yesterday I went window-shopping butcher's shop. Lawks alive, and bury me bone 🦴, dripping red blood it was (well, maybe not dripping; OK, Ma). Great sides of beef. Ohhhhh. I stood transfixed with a begging look on my face, super-Sealy stare. Did it get me anywhere? No. Entrepawneer side of me kicked in. I would block the door and not let customers in and blackmail the butcher man. I would be on my way in exchange for a juicy steak 😋. That wasn't happening, so off we trotted.

Met three nice people, one who only knew me through my posts. So had to give her an extra special display of commando crawling, which she thought was great. Also passers-by in the high street had a laugh (Ma assured me laughing with me, not at me, which would be rude). Then my new pal got her glasses out. Nearly forgot myself as I leapt up, ready for the snatch (Attitude again, not me), but Ma saw that coming, so foiled ☹. Bella, my Lab friend, who I have run around a small pocket park with no signs about, no dogs, so empty. We had a good time until I was distracted by a cat smell; they really pong. Saw a ghost cat all snowy white this morning. Scary, so left that alone.

Ma met a (wait for it) a "Doberdoodle" 😳🙀 when she went shopping without me. Ummph. She said it was bigger than my Spinone pals and was only eight months old. Giant. I will give it an earful if I see it, just to let it know who's boss. Had a play-around with my American Labrador pal. Eight stone he weighs; feel like a light weight next to him 🐶. Off for last walk now. Always look forward to bedtime, as I've got an electric blanket on my bed. Well, our bed. Snug, mmmm 🐶♡   .

28th November 2022

Misty fungal weather, as Ma would say. 😊 Good for getting filthified 😋. Hitched Ma up to her leash, and took her a country walk. If she gets muddy, I'll just have to get that water-spitting snake in my garden to clean her up. Lots of peemails, so took a long time (you see, I can't work from home), so Ma just has to put up with me working the hedgerows. Very misty zombie weather. Saw something about that in a story on the picture box. They always stumble through mist with body parts and bandages hanging off them. There she goes, spoilsport Ma, telling me, "Get a grip, young man," so I gave her leash a sharp tug 😤. That'll "larn her".

Met my new neighbours the Elites (Eite, really, but I've elevated them by adding an extra L to their surname). Had big fuss made of me when I suddenly saw a plastic container ex-cheese dip, and I pounced on that, licking like mad. I know it was empty, but I could smell it still. *Well*—rude. Ma enlisted the help of my Elite neighbours. They assaulted me and got my goody away from me. In fact, fair to say I feel quite traumatized. That was my find 😟.

Got to come back through town. Love that. I stared in all the shop doorways. Tried to go in the pubs once but got dragged out. Then met my pal Debbie, lovely postie. I started high-fiving like mad. Then I got a treat 😋, so going to have a nap now. 'Spect Attitude will take a break too and stop sitting on my shoulder, egging me on to do bad things. Happy Monday 🐶♡   .

30ᵗʰ November 2022

Another misty fungal morning. Hitched Ma up to the leash, and off we trotted. Did the country lane walk again. This time Ma took a pic of a little robin, who waited whilst she fumbled around for our phone. He was looking at us for ages, not at all worried. Eventually got her moving again.

Next thing, lawks alive, and bury me bone, terrifying sight. Evil swans flying over us. Now that was a first for me. Crossed my paws that they had been to the toilet before take-off. Can do without sights like that. Dragged Ma through town on the way back, meeting and greeting and commando crawling our way along the pavement. Person said, "Hello, are you Brock?" Ma didn't know him 😵. Wonder if he knew I was a knight of the land and my kennel club name is Magical Duke. Bit of a mouthful, so Brock will do to my friends. I digress.

Next find was what turned out to be a pasty in a bag. Swhoosh—scooped that up (humans are so wasteful). I was allowed to bring it to my front door, and then Ma swooped, size sevens stamping down on the wrapping. Then the fight. Wow, most of it landed on the top of the car's bonnet. Greasy mess 😤. Would have been better in my belly, and all I had for my hard work was a few measly crumbs. Now I call that assault.

I'm sitting on the settee doing my neighbourhood watch, thinking about it. I think I'm quite traumatized. My find, my treat. All this about "it's for your own good" a load of hogwash (Ma's expression again). Ridiculous. Who washes hogs 😯. Sure she doesn't have much of a grasp of the king's English. She's a little strange 😜. Hope she doesn't see this 😤. Have a happy Thursday, December 1ˢᵗ 🐶♡   . That was another thing Ma pinched me then punched me this morning and when I looked crossly at her she said, "It's what humans do: pinch and punch, first of the month." Can't wait for repeat performance January 1ˢᵗ 😵😖🐶♡   .

1ˢᵗ December 2022

At 12.40 a.m. Ma squeezed to the end of the bed. Just been snoring so loudly she couldn't settle. Sooo comfy—new bed linen, warm brushed cotton plus electric blanket what more can you ask for. Ma watching her picture thing she calls it a tablet. There you go again. Thought you swallowed tablets. This one so big, too big even for her mouth 😂. English language sooo complicated. Give me Welsh anytime or even double Dutch! Oops. Ma's daughter-in-law is Dutch, and grandchildren Anglo/Dutch 😂😆. Hot toddy nightcap (she's drinking it, not wearing it 😆) by her side, ready for her. Now quite awake and blaming me. Ughhh. Insomnia, that's what she calls it, whatever that means. Sounds nasty to me. Hope it's not contagious like my nemesis, that spotty dog. My spots getting bigger on my belly by the day. His fault. Well, feel quite tired after posting this. Paws aching, so I'm off again to the land of nod. Misty already outside, so lay in today, as past the bewitching hour already 😴😴😴😺♡　.

3ʳᵈ December 2022

Hi, guys. What an exciting walk I took Ma on this morning. Wet, but hey, got away without wearing that dreaded high-viz jacket Ma bought me, as dry start. Came back through town, and on the way a little elf (OK, Ma, I will call them elves just because it tickles my fancy) came up on his little trike, jumped off, and asked Ma if he could say hello to me. Proceeded to tell us his name was Oliver. (He was American. Have quite a lot, as Molesworth just up the road American intelligence.) He asked us our names, very polite and very small. Gave him my best super-Sealy grin, and Ma said Val and Brock. His dad was lovely too; thanked us very much.

Around the corner 😳🎺🎺🎺 brass band playing Xmas music and farmers market very busy and the smells, wonderful. Did I get bought anything? *No*, same old excuse; money at home. Pshhhht. Further on some people were holding some furry things, two, in fact. Guinea pigs Ma called them. Mmmmm, now they looked tasty. "*No*, you are not Peruvian," I was told very sternly by Ma (still trying to work that out). We have a cattle and sheep market every Saturday, but there's also a fur and feather market every so often. Don't think Ma's going to take me there 😆😂.

Nearly succeeded with a sandwich snatch. Literally "out of the mouths of babes and sucklings"— another of Ma's silly sayings 😊. A little girl elf was happily eating a delicious sandwich right down at my level. Ma noticed just in time. My mouth was half open thwarted again. Die of hunger at this rate ☹ 　. Met a few of my human friends who of course got commando crawling treatment, even in the wet, and then came back for bacon sarnie brunch. Well, you can imagine my size of bacon. I got a sliver lawks alive, and bury me bone 🦴, but I do get cucumber 🥒 chunks for my brunch, so not all bad. Enough Ma wants her phone back. Rude; not finished yet. Pardon, did I hear sighs of impatience? ☹ 　😆♡ 　😺

6ᵗʰ December 2022

Halt, who goes there? Just back on duty paddock playschool this morning, and I can see my friend Debbie postie. Here comes my treat through the letter box. Yum, isn't she the bestest 😺♡　.

6th December 2022, continued ...

Here is my predecessor, Angus. He was also a keen neighbourhood watchdog. Impressive, handsome boy. ♡ I wonder what he thinks of me 😵. At least carrying on the tradition 🤡🥴♡ .

8th December 2022

Well, wonderful deep frost, and sun. Couldn't stop rolling in the frost, Ma waiting. I just blamed Attitude. Said he told me to 🤪, Then I saw two ladies coming along so had to lie down and wait. Much to Ma's embarrassment, I commando crawled up to them. Yup, had them in the pad of my paw. They made such a fuss of me. They were American, and I actually kept pace with them, dragging Ma along. I think I might have mentioned this before 😵‍💫. Never mind eh.

Best walk for a long time. We walked by the river and through the woods. There in the frost white field I saw (wait for it) *penguins*. Yup, for sure. I was sooo excited. Only seen them on picture box at home. Ma, look. I ran towards them and they flew off? Ma said, "Brock, you and your imagination. They are *magpies*." Well, Attitude said they were penguins (I'll blame him as I felt embarrassed). Ma said, "They are black and white, and there, little man, that's where the similarity ends." 😵

Well, I skipped on. Saw hairy rats running up the trees. Tried to chase them. Ma said, "You've got the devil in you this morning." Huh? *Rude.* I have got enough problems having an invisible friend, Attitude, without being possessed by this devil person. Only so much a guy can take. Last night I tried to destroy Ma's big shopping bag. It made such a lovely crackly noise. Of course, *cheese.* Yup, swopped it for a bit of cheese. Not daft, me 😂🤪😺♡　　.

10ᵗʰ December 2022

Hide-and-seek 😸. Ma and I went out delivering some cards this afternoon. I got so excited going down all these paths but soon realised the doorstep was as far as we were going ☹　　. I was so looking forward to rushing in and inspecting everybody else's house (must get nosiness inherited from somewhere 😛😛😛).

Anyway, met a few pals. One was a doodle girl whose eyelashes are so long and black against her cream-coloured coat. Stunning. She said they're natural 😳. Going to have a game with her next time and try to dislodge them. Proof of the pudding and all that.

There was another cucumber heist again this evening. (When she's having her dinner I get little chunks of cucumber delicately handed to me for me to snatch away, leaving Ma's fingers in danger of amputation. No manners, I've been told.) Ma was getting one out of the fridge. There it was, dangling from Ma's hand, but not for long. Whoosh, off it went. Very hard to chew and run at the same time, but I've mastered the art. By the time the cheese exchange took place, only a third left. Yes, you guessed it. None for me this evening. Cucumber deprived 😞. Well, apart from what I stole. Attitude told me to do it. It would never have entered my head otherwise (quite handy these invisible friends🤪). Had such a fun morning frost rolling. Can't wait for tomorrow 😺♡　　.

11ᵗʰ December 2022

Kitegate 🦅. The very cheek of it. Focus on my shed roof. Yup, *chicken* put out for the kites (vultures, really, but Ma calls them kites😞). If I had giraffe legs, a ladder even. Lawks alive, and bury me bone, frustrating to say the least.

I got Ma ready for our walk. Well, she could hardly move for layered clothes topped off with a hooded coat that looks like a bear coat. If she gets mistaken for a Yeti, that's it. Last time that coat sees the light of day, with me anyway. First few minutes were taken over by rolling in the thick frosty grass (me, not Ma; she wouldn't have been able to get up 😸😸). Ohhh, it was bliss. Commando crawling around, then off I trotted, dragging Ma onwards, who trundled along, weighted down by clothes, staring in dismay at my green stained coat. Could be a trend setter, grass green fur. Inflewencing again. It got foggier. Ma was telling me 👻 ghost stories and about zombies staggering through the fog. Huh, and you wonder where I get my imagination from. Didn't frighten me though, as I'm a super-Sealy and a knight of the realm, although made to leave my sword 🗡　　at home (Ma said I'd trip over it—short legs; *Rude*).

Met a doodle girl the required colour, it would seem, chocolatey brown. She was full of fun. We cavorted around on the end of our leashes. Mind you, bit difficult with my anchor man of a Ma holding on with her thermal gloves 😔. Next along, my old pal (he's a "Jackshit" 😂😂😂😂, a Jack Russell–Shih Tzu cross). We exchanged smells, and I heard his ma telling my ma a miniature dachshund is arriving next week. I looked at my pal, who raised his eyebrows and shook his head. He already shares his house with two ginormous long-coated Siamese cats 🙀. Yuk. Ma likes dachsies; calls them sausage dogs. Well, the size of this newcomer, he'd have to be classed as a cocktail sausage. Certainly not frankfurter size. Can't wait to meet him, although Ma said not to hurt his back. As if I was rough and clumsy—*really*. Hope you have all had a good Sunday and stayed warm. Arrivederci (ciao—studying Italian so I can converse with my Spinone pals) 🤍 🐵.

13ᵗʰ December 2022

Hey, hope all is well. Not hiring Ma out for any wedding videos any time soon 🙄. She can even start a video normally, and halfway through, it goes to slo-mo 😵. Lawks alive, and bury me bone, I could do a better job.

Paddock playschool this morning. Still bit of snow about. Very cold but great fun. Just come back from early afternoon walk before it freezes. Went through the woods, and saw one bird so still and quiet—spooky 👻. Attitude whispered in my ear, "Let's spook Ma for a laugh." I suddenly sprang to attention, back legs splayed out(my hunting stance looks authentic, but only ever hunted for food—oh, and cats of course). My schnozzle was pointed into the woods. I froze like a statue, full alert, wouldn't move, transfixed to the spot 😂😂. Did the trick. Ma watches too much scary stuff on the picture box. It would be fair to say her imagination is more than mine. And she wonders where I get it from. Don't stand a chance do I?

Anyway, eventually moved on, keeping Ma on a short leash. Didn't want her to go skittering off into the undergrowth. Met my humendous Dobermann pal on the way, desperate for a game. We were both leaping around, but Ma said it was too icy to cavort about. Did just a bit; couldn't resist. Our car is at the mot man's garage today, hopefully it gets through, and I'm not asked to give up my treats to help pay a huge bill 😵. I know it's my car but ...

15ᵗʰ December 2022

Little elf Fiadh visited. Reeeeealy great. There was food on the scene. I got dropped bits—yum. Not one but three dummy heists. Ha, thought I'd forgotten. Not a chance. Fiadh's ma, Megan, had put her coat on the settee, so when nobody was looking, Attitude told me to look in her pocket. Eureka. Lawks alive, and bury me bone (could see cheddar cheese on the horizon here😂), out it came, and off I flew. Sure enough, Ma running around shouting *Cheese!* 🐭. Exchange was made. Big display of sterilizing the dummy. *Rude* and hurtful, I thought. Second time Fiadh dropped it, and third time, wee, she sort of threw it at me. (Well, that's my story, and I'm sticking to it.) I think my little elf was enjoying this game. She now has the most sterile dummy ever 🙄. Must admit she tasted very nice. Good old face wash was in order, though the big humans didn't think much to it. Hmmmph; don't care. 😵. It was crowded on grandad's (which he is now) knee, my elf and me both. Later exceeded all expectations. I made off with a wee-wee nappy (had to put that in so you know I wasn't being too gross 😅). The cheese was being well used today 😂 just the tiniest bit, because of weight gain 😵.

Morning walk was a three-cat walk. First was a static cat, so just walked past, but, oh, if they move, that's it. So bit of a leash twister there. Eventually got Ma to calm down. Lots of frost and a bit of snow about, so Ma was allowed to stand at the end of the extended leash, on trust not to move, whilst I rolled, commando crawled, and head ploughed through it. Glorious.

More Xmas card deliveries. More disappointment, as nobody appeared. Ah, well, back home. A good Friday so far ♡ 🤡. Stay safe and warm. Signing off, Magical Duke and Sir Brock—have to remind myself sometimes I'm titled.

17th December 2022

Nice walk yesterday. Still a bit of frosty snow. About to head surf. Met up with my Airedale lady friend. We had a quick shuffle game, and on we went through the woods. Guess who I saw. I saw Rudolph. Really so excited, although his nose wasn't red. Of course got corrected. "No, Brock, it's a muntjac deer." OK, Ma (spoilsport). He was quite a way away from us and disappeared into the wood before I could give chase. Make a change from cats and hairy rats. We also came across a huge corpse frozen solid, a snarl on its face, its glowing red eyes staring menacingly into space 😜. Would I be allowed to carry it back home? Better than empty crisp bags that I'm usually landed with, and my street cred would rise to giddy heights. Could pretend I'd caught it 😅. Ma said no, definitely not. Leave the poor little 😳 —yes, little mouse where it was. She spoils my adventures sometimes; no imagination. She was on local radio the other day talking to the gardening man. Advice about her fruit trees. Ummmmph. I wanted in on this radio thing. I could tell him all about the watering of plants and trees. Irrigating Sealy, that's me, and I pull plants out of the pots if needs be. But no, I got told, hush. Rude. I wanted to say hi to all my pals too, but no such luck. Ah, well, it's raining now. One happy thought—spa day tomorrow. Sooo if it's dirty weather, I will filthify quicker 🤡♡ 😂.

21st December 2022

Hi, there. Just got time to paw this out. Sooo busy, lawks alive, and bury me bone. First was the spa day. Sparkling white ☹ afternoon walk. I was smelt by one of my pals, and he told me I smelt terrible. He cocked his nose in the air and gave an enormous sneeze. Rude! Made me jump sky high. Thought he'd gone into internal combustion, and it would have been all my fault. Attitude was smirking, I imagine, as I can't see him. He loves getting me into trouble.

Then before paddock playschool we had a visitor, Lynne, who had worked with Ma at the surgery. Xmas card delivering. Well, she had never met me or Miss Ziggy Stardust. She was very nice and let me jump on her knee and wash her with sloppy Sealy kisses. I enjoyed it; hope she did 😂. Then my transport arrived for playschool. Ohhh, the excitement. Off I dashed, flinging a warbling byeee to Lynne (she was probably glad to see me go 😂). I got Xmas cards and pressy from Dani and Emma who run playschool. And please note, my pressy was a fridge magnet with my name on it. It is now officially my fridge (it always was, really). Now no argument. Course I let Ma use it too.

Well, had a nice walk this morning with a visiting spaniel on holiday here with one of Ma's friends. She was very nice, with long eyelashes, and I told my mates who I saw that she was my girlfriend (white Sealy lie 😂). Filthified, yeah, black legs dirty. Rainy weather, and as for my belly 😂, Ma cringes every time I commando crawl. Had treats from postie Debbie outside the post office. Then later as post came through the door, another treat—lucky me. Have a lovely day 🤡♡ .

22nd December 2022

I am very concerned. Lawks alive, and bury me bone, how is Father Xmas coming to *me* 😣☹ ☹ ? Look what Ma did to our chimney. Blocked it off. Crimes, I hope he doesn't come down and get stuck behind the boarding. Ma said it's OK because every time I look in that fire thingy, a Sealy looks back at me, even through the flames, and he will hear Father Xmas and shout a Sealy warning, and he'll leave all my presents by the back door. Phew, that's a relief.

Well, what a sight. Beggars belief. There's Ma tucking away into a plate of tapeworms again (she calls it spaghetti) 😂, and they are red in colour. Nearly putting me off my food—nearly. Takes a lot. Mmmmm, have to get stuff from my doctor's to dose her.

Played a great joke on Ma this afternoon. I lifted my left leg against a lamp post. Quickly changed my mind—right leg up, peemail over Ma's booted toe 🤣😂. She didn't see the funny side of it. Poor sense of humour Ma's got. I was in mid-toilet mode this morning when suddenly there was the. most awful screeching snarling growling noise. So loud, and it sent my hackles up. Ma said, "It's a catfight." Never heard the likes, and how rude to disturb a chap in mid-toilet. (Ma said change the subject it's all rather lavatorial and in quite bad taste this post.)

Sooooo foggy, damp, mild, and mucky weather. Mucky I celebrate. Hope you are well. Dinner time 😆 for me, and I won't be having tapeworms ♡   🐶.

25ᵗʰ December 2022

Well, that's it. Have to wait till August for more pressies on my birthday 😎. I had such an exciting day and such lovely pressies. Thank you, everybody. Even got Xmas cards. Attitude also had loads of cards and pressies, all as invisible as him 🤭. Ziggy had a warm Xmas morning bath and a little something to eat before disappearing back to bed again 🐾. She had a moan, as Ma hadn't got any mistletoe. Uhhhh, was she angling for a lick off moi 🙀? Methinks not😌.

We had a very strange thing for Xmas dinner. Ma said it was a two-bird roast 👀. Lawks alive, and bury me bone, turkey *and* chicken 😕. I spent half the day wondering how a turkey managed to swallow a whole chicken. Their beaks must be hinged like a snake's that can swallow huge things (saw that on the picture box). And bearing in mind the fledgling incident in the spring 😟. I had to spit it out. Scratching around in my mouth; yuck. Also this is cannibalism, birds eating each other. Disgusting if there is such a word. If not I just made it up 😹. It tasted great, anyway. Enjoyed that, and I had a thing called a pig in a blanket. Once again bafflement. Bore no resemblance to any pig I've ever seen, and blankets—that's what I have in my daybed. Humans do have some funny goings-on and don't speak king's English well. It's a puzzlement at times. Glad I'm a Sealy. Mastering English is far more difficult than Italian, French, and doodle. I have a smattering of cat and horse and am learning to swear in said languages 😹. That's a secret from Ma 🙈🙈🙈🙈. Enjoy your Boxing Day. There you go again 🥊🥊🥊🥊. Am I expected to fight something or someone today? 🤪😜♡   🐶

30ᵗʰ December 2022

I get blamed for everything ☹️   . Can I help it if Ma's stupid old slipper boot followed me downstairs and on to the settee, invading my space at my watchdog post? No, not my fault 😕. Again I bet it's that darned invisible friend I'm lumbered with, Attitude. Must admit, though, today I have played up I was being totally ignored. *Rude*, wouldn't you say? Ma was on my mobile for ages. I was neglected. Hmmmm, yes. Neglected not too strong a word. Sooooo 🤪. yes. the old slipper boot heist 😹. Snatched again, closely followed by the toilet roll basket with toilet rolls scattered. Then a parcel "fell" off the table, and I helped to open it. How did I know it was ready for posting? Offered to rewrap it, but got ignored *again*. and on it went 😹😹.

Earlier this morning I found a skeleton in the garden. I thought it was a baby 🦕 dinosaur. Of course Ma played it down. Said it was a baby fledgling from springtime. Fascinating. It was intact. She could have let me keep it, as it didn't smell, but oh no—no more corpse collections allowed. It would have looked lovely framed and might have been worth a lot of money.

I put Ma's leash on, and off we trotted. I was rudely interrupted mid peemail sniffing to be told to "Put a spurt on". If I knew what a spurt was, I would have done just that to keep her happy, no matter how daft it looked on me. "Oh, Brock, it means to hurry up," I was told. Ummph. She had an appointment and needed me to "shake a leg". Think she's bonkers, all these stupid sayings. Anyway, I shook a leg and "spurted" on for the rest of my walk 😊. Human language, so hard to learn. Never going to major in this, so will put more energies into my cat and Welsh lessons. Also doodle language, as the doodles have different accents. Just deciding shall I be a good dog tonight 😕? Maybe I'll give her a break ♡ 🐶.

31st December 2022

Lawks alive, and bury me bone, she's got me in a camouflage harness. Hope I'm not called to war, but I'm nearly a commando anyway as I am always commando crawling. So be it. This morning we were prancing down the road (I was the one prancing 😄), Ma in tow. I was feeling quite the lad in my new outfit, when all of a sudden a hairy rat 🐿️ landed right in front of me and hopped across the road 😳 Crikey, if I'd been a bit further on, it might have landed on my head, and I'd look as though I was wearing a Davy Crockett hat. Beggars belief, cheek of it. Gave chase, but of course it vanished out of sight—disappeared just like that.

Looking up in the sky, the vultures (that Ma calls kites) were circling overhead. Bit of a worry they were tracking us, so I kept moving, flicking my ears back and jiggling around, just to let them know I was still breathing and not their breakfast. Then we came across a nice man washing his car, who gave me lovely strokes behind my ears. Had to stand on back legs, mind, as there was a wall between us. Then met Harry the golden Lab, who always has to smell me from head to toe and then licks me all over. Quite enjoy that 😄. Then crossing the road on the zebra crossing, which bears no resemblance to a zebra apart from the black-and-white stripes which are wearing off anyway 😊. Sooo disappointed when Ma first said let's go down to the zebra crossing when I was just a pup. I nearly ran, expecting to see a herd of zebras crossing. Disillusioned doesn't even cut it 😞 .

Over the road we met a young Westie pup. I let him jump up and sniff me. His owner said what a good pup he was, so duty-bound, I whispered into his ear, "Go for the shoes. The insoles are the things to rip out." I gave him quite a few naughty tips. He looked at me wide-eyed and squeaked back, "Thank you, soldier," looking at me with great respect (that was ref to my new camouflage harness).

I met my nemesis this morning. Boy, did I give it a mouthful, just because I can. Ma said I was bad for mouthing obscenities in the road like that, showing her up. Of course "spotted wonder boy" just trotted past, ignoring me. Arghhhh, waste of breath. Well, must prepare for wet afternoon walk and high winds (the weather, not me or Ma😄). New Year's Eve tonight. Stay safe, guys, and don't worry about the flash-bangs. Speak to you next year, and have a good evening 🐶♡ .

1st January 2023

Well, happy 1st January 2023. Lawks alive, bury me bone, night out with the boys, *never again.*

1ˢᵗ January 2023, continued ...

Had good walk this morning. Met some of my human pals. Great fusses and chats. Yes, have mastered a bit of human in my language skills, *and* didn't pull Ma flat on her face in a cat chase 😁. Nearly, but she held her ground. Well done, Ma. She dug her size sevens in, counterbalancing my enormous super-Sealy strength. Had warning words with an English bull terrier before he could tear me limb from limb (or try 😂). Of course wearing my new army camouflage harness, so I looked pretty scary anyway. Been promoted now right up to Field Marshall. Only had my uniform for a day. Quick, wasn't it? (All in the Sealy mind, of course 😁.)

Ma's best friend Auntie Pat came visiting. She had lots of Sealy kisses cos I hadn't seen her for a while. Ma didn't tell her where my beard and nose had been on my walk. Thought better of it. She had come for some medicine 🍸. She and Ma like to take medicine together. Is this legal? No pills involved, just liquid, and Ma said it's a social thing. Must be 🤔. Another strange human habit. Ohhh, it makes them loud and laughy 😵, but I get away with murder, so carry on, ladies. Fill your boots (another one of Ma's weird expressions 😵).

Whenever Ma has visitors, after I have licked them all over their face and bounced forcefully on their knee, I like to get my chew bones out and have a good old chew or get up to mischief whilst they get sillier. (I record what they are saying AND am going at some future date blackmail them should get a few bloody steaks off them. *Not swearing*, Ma, OK?) I hope you have all had a good New Year's Day. Hopefully no fireworks tonight. Paws crossed 🐶♡ .

1st January 2023, continued ...

Hatgate. The saying, "if you want to get ahead, get a hat"—well, don't think it's going to work for me. Hmmmmmph 😔🐶♡🐶.

3rd January 2023

You pesky hairy rat 🐿 , I'll get you. Lawks alive, and bury me bone, you nearly landed on my head the other day. Reckon you are the terrorist rat who had escaped from rodent rehab centre based in our woods. You're chancing your luck with super-Sealy me, and I'm in army uniform now, so I'm even tougher than before (if that's possible). Paddock playschool this morning. Came back really filthified 😂. So pleased about that. After a thorough rub-down and self-cleansing on the towel on the floor, finished off surfing the furniture. Job done.

Ma went out foraging after seeing to me. (Why doesn't she just say shopping? *And* it's not always for food!). As long as it's not my treat money she's spending, we are all right. She took the Xmas wreath off the front door as she came back in and left it on the floor 😵 while she put her shopping away. Won't she ever learn 🙄? So I very carefully started to take it to pieces. This was great. Ma oblivious to the fact until I trotted in with gold sparkly branches in my mouth, scattering glitter everywhere. The look on her face was worth it 😂. "BRO-O-O-OCK!" (Who, me? Doubt it. It was Attitude, my invisible friend, that did it.) I was told I was going to be three this August and to pull my britches up (another of Ma's silly sayings as I don't even wear any).

What that has to do with anything I don't know. Then I was told I'm not a pup anymore ☹ . Well, actually, Ma, Sealies are clowns, so live with it. Once again my offer to help rebuild the sorry-looking wreath was refused. Well, I do try, and they say God loves a trier, and I know for a fact I'm *very* trying. Good job Ma loves me so much 😍🤡♡ .

4th January 2023

I have decided that if Ma clings to the side of the bed, might as well join her. Must be good if she's doing it. Now complaints coming, as Ma can't stretch her legs. King-size bed, and we are both occupying a mere strip of it. Mind you, I crawl up later, as I curl up against her to protect her from any dangers. My bed is one of my fave places, especially when my electric blanket is on.

Well, lovely walk this morning. Met lots of pals, and made a few more. Not a doodle in sight. Most we met were very impressed with my new army camouflage harness. One little dachshund even tried to salute me 😂. Yup, he fell over. Mustn't laugh. He was showing respect, and it was very muddy. River Nene flooding. Evil swans giving me warning glances. Well, on arrival home I had a good shake in the hall 😂. Spread the mud splatters, then frog marched (thought they hopped; Ma again with her silly sayings) through to yard. Uh-uh, this does not bode well at all. Sure enough, black water-spitting snake turned on 😂😂😂😂. Frost had split its mouth. Water sprayed in every direction but not on me. Ma got a faceful, and I was standing pressed flat against the back door, dry and filthified. I didn't escape though, as Ma was determined even though she was soaked, so I got hosed down, *but* so did Ma—straight in the face all over her hair. Ohhhh, if only I'd had my camera. So who had last laugh? Brocky boy, methinks 😂🤡♡ .

5th January 2023

Really, just how am I supposed to get Ma out for her afternoon walk? Workmen are digging up my path (fibre-optic cables, Ma said—whatever 🙄). They've been in every road in town, and now it's my turn. Fascinated; not one Sealy bark has passed my lips. Strangely enough, glued to my post, observing. Must inspect later and make sure they haven't unearthed any bones.

Last night watching the picture box fantastic programme just for me called *Dogs Behaving Very Badly*. I lay by Ma on the settee, picking up all the very worst habits of these doggy rebels for use when I run out of my own personal store. They are my heroes and mentors 😄. Ma said, "Beware, you might be on there next." Lawks alive, and bury me bone, *yes* please. You see, I do go mad with joy when visitors arrive, jumping so high up and down, but fair to say, when they do battle through, collapsing onto the settee, hair awry, clothes hanging off them in a dishevelled state, I'm right on their lap, giving them a thorough Sealy wash to revive them, except the odd few who are allergic to my charms. Then I'm made to stay on the floor (of course they are probably in shock). Same performance when they go, but by then I'm out in the garden, so they can scramble their way out as fast as possible. Can't see their heels for dust. The braver ones do return.

7th January 2023

I'm an official watchdog here. Fancy Fiadh's outfit: bunny on the front and big one on her bum. Very tempting when she crawls away 😸. Pity there's no bunny Maltesers like I find in the fields. Ah, well, can't have everything. Managed a sock heist from her, though, but dummies weren't available this time.

Later I hitched Ma up to our leash, and we sallied forth. Met some pals, who all admired my new army outfit, *and* I've got a matching collar now (belt and braces, but I'm an escape artist; just another trick I have. I can twist and wriggle out of my harness 😆). Met Alfie, one of my BFs, and he gave me a lovely greeting, jumping around, wagging his tail, so we had a little game. He was impressed with my army rig, and when I whispered to him I'm now a field marshal, he nodded his head sagely and said, "I knew you were always destined for great things" (somebody said maliciously; jealous I guess!). "If you are who you say you are, you'd have a batman." So I told him, "Yes, I have Corporal Attitude (my invisible friend). He's wearing his invisibility cloak— undercover, as it happens." Gave a snort, tossed one of my ears nonchalantly over my neck, and marched off. I wore my last harness out commando crawling for people, so think Ma's getting me another one as well. She's got loads of clothes, so why not me too?

I can whistle now apparently. I will never hear it as Ma said I only do it in my sleep. I've tried to purse my lips contorting my face. Impossible, so I must be a nose whistler (good job Ma doesn't do it; size of her schnozzle, it would break the sound barrier 😂). Just got told not to be so rude. Who, moi? Never ♡ 🐶.

8th January 2022

Busy weekend visiting Auntie Pat's. Yesterday saw me perched on top of her chair, perfecting my balancing act. Great fun digging all her cushions out of the settees (Mollie's fault, as she buries her biscuits under them). Well, got quite a few biscuits. Thinking of Mollie's waistline really. Then 🙀🙀🙀 Attitude, my invisible friend, told me to do something soooo naughty. Mollie's teddy bear was lying on the floor. I gave it a good sniff and left a peemail on it. Lawks alive, and bury me bone, Ma was mortified. Nearly hit the roof overreacting as usual, and Auntie Pat didn't mind (so she said). Out came the special bottle with magic stuff inside that is used for just this sort of horror happening. Can't say accident, can you, as you can't peemail by accident 😵. Anyway, all cleared up. Humans back to their medicine dosing, *and* they devoured best part of a box of chocs right in front of Mollie and me. Gluttons, these humans and they talk about me. Hmmmph.

Last night on the picture box was a programme on the moors, and I looked up from bone chewing as I heard the cry of a vulture kite. There was one swooping across the screen. I leapt up and dashed into the back room. running around. staring at the ceiling, which Ma thought was hilarious 😂. Of course I was only pretending, just to amuse her (well, that's my story, and I'm sticking to it).

Something that really puzzles me is when Ma's groomer comes every week. She really seems to enjoy it. Hairdryer blowing on, brushing going on, hmmmm. Take myself off to watchdog duties.

Aren't humans strange, and they're always washing themselves, showering, and bathing. Yuck and double yuck. Makes me feel quite nauseous.

Did well on this morning's walk. Passed the charity shop, and went up the steps, staring through the door, forlorn brown eyes and big black schnozzle pressed on the glass. (I am allowed back in after the shoplifting affair when I helped myself to a fluffy slipper 😂.) The lady came out with some treats for me 😊 (nobody's fool, me 😅). The picture of me is just after I plundered a sandwich off Ma's plate, and I'm looking at her with my best pleading expression and "I'm starving" eyes, which didn't work. She just called me a thieving Sealy. *Rude*, no call for that. Well, I am off. Out for second walk. Don't have to muzzle Ma now, as I've put her on trust. Paws crossed she behaves; time will tell. Hope you all had a good weekend. Ciao for now 🐶♡ .

10th January 2023

Day off from field marshalling today, guys. I'm in the construction industry, high-viz. Pleaded with Ma for a hard hat, but told, "No, Brock, it would fall over your eyes." 🙄 End of that conversation. I sort of blend in too with the men who have dug up my path at the end of the drive. Now filled in, but gloriously mudified, all for the sake of something called fibre-optics for broadband or something like that. Walking past today, they were drilling away, and I got smiles and greetings from them. We all had high-viz gear on, but the men on the drills had ear defenders on. Pleeeease, Ma, please can I have some of those things? No, again. Head too narrow now—always an excuse.

Met a little spaniel who looked me up and down, staring at my uniform. He sidled up to my ear (after our usual botty sniffs) and whispered, "Where are you working, and what have you built?" Well, my friend, just completed building a huge castle in never land heights. Of course I was project manager (overseeing it). That's why my high-viz gear is so clean (for now 😂). I also told him I am a knight of the realm, knighthood bestowed on me by my Spinone pal, performed spontaneously on the pavement with a crowd of five passers-by in the audience a while ago now. Crikey he was so impressed he asked me if he could come some of the walk with Ma and me. I looked over my shoulder at Ma. She was behaving well today. Just raised my eyebrows and gave her my super-Sealy stare, warning her in my way, *Behave*. Hope tomorrow Ma dresses me in my camo gear like that better.

Met my new friends this morning: Sue, her nice husband, and Helen, her sister. So commando crawled for them, webbing of my new gear dragging along the ground. Ma's face, listening to my new expensive outfit grinding away 😂—amazing. I received a Xmas card today. Late cos of mail strike. Just my name and address; no town, no postcode. And my pal Debbie delivered it today 😳. So today through the letterbox was my own mail addressed to me 📨 plus my Bonio biscuit. Yeeea, result. Off now for final walk of the day, then *dinner* 😋🐶♡ . P.S. Ma's mail was all rubbish 😂.

11th January 2023

Baby me not been here a week. Puppy labour, gardening assistant already And so it began 🐶♡ .

14th January 2023

Morning. Well, what can I say? Drenched today. Mariamman (Hindu goddess of rain) visited us with a vengeance. (Ma said it's good for my education to learn these things and names – of course it is will come in soooo handy with my exchanges with my pals 🥱🥱🥱; bore them rigid. Hmmmm, home schooling 😕😊) Anyway, ventured out sporting my dreaded wet weather coat. Rain was slashing down, Ma getting soaked, whilst I was dry as a bone. Underneath the hedge 😄 checked out all my peemails, as they hadn't been washed away yet. We walked down the hill, then the hedge came to an end, and I had to expose my Sealy body to the elements. I hate getting wet (only exception is paddock playschool). Met my cavalier King Charles mate Theodore. He was dripping wet 💧💧💧. He muttered a disgruntled "Whatcha, mate?" (Speaks a bit commonly with such a fancy name and bloodline.) So I tossed an ear over my soaking wet shoulder and said, "Bonjour, ma petit chien," summoning up my pitiful knowledge of the French Ma had taught me, and sauntered off, leaving Theodore dripping wet with a puzzled look on his face 😄. I have promised Ma she can go a longer walk this afternoon, as it's clearing up. She didn't look as thrilled as I hoped she would.

I have been told by Ma to watch my language in my posts as I have to be "woke" 😊. *Really*. Course I'm awake; don't do this in my sleep, do I? Though very proud of being able to whistle in my sleep. Yup, Ma said not through my pursed lips. Can't do that (had to give up my oboe lessons cos couldn't purse my lips). I nose whistle. Now I'm going to ask Ma to help me do it whilst I'm conscious, and maybe through my entrepawneeral skills make us some money. I can see my name in lights: BROCK HILDITCH, THE ONLY WHISTLING SEALYHAM IN THE WORLD. What fame and hopefully fortune could be had, and Ma could keep me in the manner I would like to be accustomed to: rump steak, a whole salmon, great big bones, mmmmmm. List goes on.

Enough waffling on. Going to hitch Ma up and drag her out again. Hope your Saturdays have been dryer and that Mariamman has stayed away from you. Keep Ma happy; used the rain goddess's name again, though will have forgotten it in thirty minutes 😂♡🤡.

14ᵗʰ January 2023, continued ...

Yuck 🙁. Wind howling, bed warm. Out there, cold. Oh,OK, you win, Ma. So up we rose. Breakfast for me, cuppa for Ma, beard brush (me, not Ma, although 😅?). Why, I don't know. It's a morning ritual. I like it all curly and macho. Then I hitched her up to my leash and sallied forth. Aeolus, god king of winds (my Greek studies coming in handy), was buffeting us back and forth. Lawks alive, and bury me bone, something had really upset him. Wind whistling through telegraph wires, gusting, bringing us both up short. So head down, boyo, and did my husky impression, and dragged Ma along. Well, must say she was being very difficult. Every way I wanted to go, oh no, and she was pulling the other way. But guess who won 😇. So I dragged her past the lakes and the river, which was running very fast, so extra careful she didn't fall in, as she'd left her water wings at home (so disorganized). The woman can't swim, can't even get up a fast paddle, I'm told. I'm terrified every time she has a shower at home. The evil swans giving me leery looks, and the ducks' feathers all ruffled with the wind. Sympathies there. My eyebrows were lashing round my head.

And off to the next village, whereupon I stopped and waited for passers-by to catch up to say good morning and present my head for an ear rub. Gets them every time—big brown eyes, big black schnozzle, and waggy tail—but of course Ma was getting very fed up, and that silly phrase "Shake a leg" 😵 rang in my ears, so shook all four, but not before doing a commando crawl, scraping my new harness along the ground 😖. That'll teach you, I thought, and so we carried on.

Met a—you guessed it—a doodle of some sort. Always up for a game, so we had a dance around. Must say they are fun. Far up the road I saw the pug boys out with their ma. They are very solid, so no danger of an updraft carrying them off. Eventually we got back, dry for once, hmmmph, with clean paws 😔 (hate being clean). Rain forecast for tomorrow, so I will get gloriously filthified again 😹😹. Friday the thirteenth was a doddle, but of course, paws crossed, not midnight yet ♡🤡.

15ᵗʰ January 2023

Stop press! I have just received a peemail from Green Clown face 🤡😸. We are true peemail pals, and I'm going to be busy being a full-time peemail correspondent, and as Ma always tells me, at the end of the day, it's all about the schnozzle 👃.

Signing off for now, and hope you have enjoyed my take on life. And don't forget it is all about schnozzle.